CLOWNS *of the* HOPI

CLOWNS
of the HOPI

Tradition Keepers and Delight Makers

by

BARTON WRIGHT

with illustrations by the author and

photographs by

JERRY JACKA

NORTHLAND PUBLISHING

First Edition, 1994

ISBN 0-87358-572-0

Library of Congress Catalog Card Number Pending

Frontispiece: The figure on the left is very similar to the
Tachukti, the indigenous form of the Koyemsi. He is a
Toson or Sweet-Cornmeal-Tasting Koyemsi, as is the
more contemporary one to his right. (left) Herbert
Talaheftewa, Shungopovi, 1960–1970. 9" E. Lowry Collection.
(right) Jonathan Day, Hotevilla, 1983. 11" S. Simpson Collection.

This page: Koshari or Tewa clown during a Long Hair
dance at Sichomovi in 1919. (Courtesy of Anna Kopta and
University of New Mexico Photo Archives)

Design by Larry Lindahl
Manufactured in Hong Kong by Wing King Tong

0471/7.5M/6-94

CONTENTS

PREFACE

THERE ARE MANY REASONS FOR WRITING A BOOK ON CLOWNS. An enchanting phenomenon, clowns have always fascinated people—some want to be one, others just want to know about them. All groups of people have some version of the clown figure, and the types of clowns and amount of literature associated with them are extensive. However, what on the surface seems to be a simple subject becomes complex when explored in greater depth.

The Hopi, who are so amply supplied with clowns, have received scant attention. In addition, much of the information that does exist is inadequate. The purpose of this book is to identify and illustrate those personages the Hopi consider (either historically or modern-day) to be clowns and those that they do not. The book also illustrates how the Hopi carver presents these figures as dolls, or *tihus*. Where possible and appropriate, the various clowns' purposes and historical backgrounds are given as best as can be determined by a non-Hopi outsider.

The information presented here has been accumulated over a period of nearly forty years of attendance at dances; conversations with many Hopi friends; photographs; art; and the writings of early observers. Few of these individuals were trained in the new field of anthropology, instead they happened to be on the scene at the right time and interested enough to record those observations. Alexander M. Stephen was in Keams Canyon because of an interest in mining, but he left behind the most comprehensive document written on the Hopi. The Reverend H. R. Voth was a Mennonite missionary who believed that change to a better religion could be accomplished only if one knew what the Hopi believed, so he wrote of his findings. The prolific writer J. Walter Fewkes incorporated much of Stephen's findings, as did Cosmo Mindeleff, in his published material. However, he and the romantic Frank Hamilton Cushing were the only nineteenth-century observers with even a modicum of training. The other eminent writer of that era was Matilda Coxe Stevenson, whose opportunity consisted of being the wife of an Army man assigned to make an expedition into the region. Although she wrote extensively on Zuni and the Zia, it will never be known which were her husband's observations and which were hers.

In an interesting twist, many of the writers of the early twentieth century were women trained in the field of anthropology and who had specific goals. Elsie Clews Parsons, with her interest in the role of women in other cultures, probably wrote more on a greater number of Pueblo cultures than any other author. Ruth Bunzel, Esther Goldfrank, Ruth Benedict, Laura Thompson, and Gladys Reichard all left reports dealing with subject matter ranging from poetry and painting to folklore and social structure.

A list of other trained ethnologists and anthropologists who worked among the Pueblo people reads like a roll call of well-known scientists: Kroeber, Lowie, Eggan, White, Titiev to name but a few. All of these individuals left invaluable data for those who are interested.

There are several museums whose collections house some of the most valuable information available on Pueblo cultures. These include the American Museum of Natural History (New York, New York); Brooklyn Museum (Brooklyn, New York); Carnegie Museum of Natural History, Carnegie Institute (Pittsburgh, Pennsylvania); Field Museum of Natural History (Chicago, Illinois); Maxwell Museum of Anthropology (Albuquerque, New Mexico); Milwaukee Public Museum (Milwaukee, Wisconsin); *Museum fur Volkerkunde* (Berlin/Dahlem, Germany); Smithsonian Institution (Washington, D.C.); Museum of New Mexico, Laboratory of Anthropology (Santa Fe, New Mexico); San Diego Museum of Man (San Diego, California); Southwest Museum (Los Angeles, California); and University of Colorado Museum (Boulder, Colorado).

There is, however, another source, particularly for the Hopi, that is often overlooked. It is the work of the many anonymous kachina carvers whose dolls repose in numerous museums across this country and Europe. An untapped history, these dolls are the unwritten documentation of change, of evolving art forms, of shifting attitudes, of losses and gains, and of artistic license. To all of the above individuals, both known and unknown, a debt of gratitude is owed by all who benefit from their works.

I would like to end with a most heartfelt thanks to Jane Metzger, without whose initial support for the research on kachina dolls in museum collections, little would have been accomplished.

INTRODUCTION

ACROSS AMERICA WORD SPREADS THAT "THE CIRCUS IS COMING to town and it is going to have clowns!" or "There is going to be a parade with clowns!" and excitement builds as images of absurd costumes, ridiculous faces, and amusing antics spring immediately to mind. The very word *clown* predisposes us to laughter and amusement, an attitude honed by generations of exposure to these actors. Without doubt, comic figures have been a part of human life since the first pratfall produced laughter, but through the ages they have served many other purposes as well.

Clowning as a profession began in ancient Greece with secondary figures in farces, padded and bald-headed buffoons who parodied the actions of the actors. Their mirth-producing behavior continued long after the Greek theaters had disappeared into antiquity and, in due time, became the stock-in-trade of the traveling minstrel of the Middle Ages. With the advent of Amateur Fool Societies and the appearance of various specialties, clowning became a vocation.

The Italians gave us Harlequin, the comic valet and subordinate who slowly developed into an acrobatic trickster. The English clown who appeared around Shakespearean times in medieval mystery plays became a buffoon and prankster whose sly wit could deceive even the devil. France gave us the tragic white-faced clown, Pierrot, but it was seventeenth-century Germany that gave us the traditional costume of baggy clothes and oversized feet. The first true circus clown, Grimaldi, came on the scene around the beginning of the nineteenth century with a repertoire of acrobatic tumbling, pratfalls, and slapstick. Modern clowns—Emmett Kelly, the Vagabond Clown, and Charlie Chaplin, the Little Clown—retained the oversized feet, baggy costumes, and white faces we regard as characteristic of clowns, and their sole purpose was to amuse us.

But not all clowns are purely for amusement. A slightly different type of clown, the jesters, developed in the royal courts of the Middle Ages. Their purpose was somewhat different from that of ordinary clowns, for they played a double role. Not only did they act the buffoon to amuse their royal audiences; they could also offer unwelcome advice in the guise of non-aggressive humor. In this regard, the jester was not unlike a sacred or ritual clown.

Most pre-literate cultures have clowns who behave in a manner similar to the jester, giving unsolicited advice through the medium of humor. However, the role of these clowns is far more complex than that of the court fool because, in addition to offering humor and advice, they are often believed to be quasi-inhabitants of the supernatural world or to personify beings from there. Such clowns are therefore sacred and are a combination of jester, priest, and shaman.

In a single performance, the sacred clowns can serve many purposes. Their "play" can offer a psychotherapeutic release for the audience through amusement. At the same time, they may intensify a ritual in progress by contrasting the sublime and the ridiculous. They can also control non-conformist behavior in either groups or individuals through comic object lessons, as well as avert evil or the actions of witches. These outrageous actions—performing what is essentially a dangerous departure from acceptable behavior—must be sanctioned in some fashion by the group. In consequence, it is usually believed that they are representatives of some powerful primordial being with whom they interact.

The powers of the supernatural patrons may vary, but even between seemingly unrelated peoples, they often have a common purpose. Hence, while the role of the sacred clowns themselves varies slightly, and ranges from a single goal to complex multiple aims, ultimately their empowered actions exercise a considerable degree of control, having an impact on all individuals within a given village, and transecting every organization.

CLOWNS *of the* HOPI

AN OVERVIEW

Above: Koyemsi entering the plaza over the rooftops and over the spectators as well.

Courtesy of John Wilson

Left: A Kaisale is playing ball and, if the look on his face is any indication, the catcher is in trouble. The carver made two, one catching and one throwing, but unfortunately the dolls have been separated.

Jim Fred, Bakavi, year unknown. 17"
Frank and Patricia Marie Collection.

Within the Southwestern region of the United States, there is a cluster of distinct Indian tribes known as the Pueblo people, the village dwellers, who have a well-developed clown system. These different villages share a community of philosophical concepts, religious beliefs, and practices. The neighboring non-Pueblo tribes may at times display superficial similarities of belief but in general, they represent a greater departure than will be found between the Pueblo villages.

However, the Pueblo people themselves are not a homogeneous unit. Six separate linguistic groups are represented in more than thirty different New Mexico and Arizona villages. The easternmost settlements are the Tiwan pueblos of Taos and Picuris. Below Taos, near the junction of the Chama and the Rio Grande, are the Tewa pueblos of San Juan, Santa Clara, San Ildefonso, Nambé, and Tesuque. Farther south are the Keresan pueblos of Cochiti, Santo Domingo, Santa Ana, and Zia.

Near the tiny San Jose River lie the other Keresan villages of Acoma and Laguna. Along the middle Rio Grande are the two lower Tiwan villages of Sandia and Isleta, while on the northwestern edge of the Keresan pueblos along the Jemez River is the Towan town of

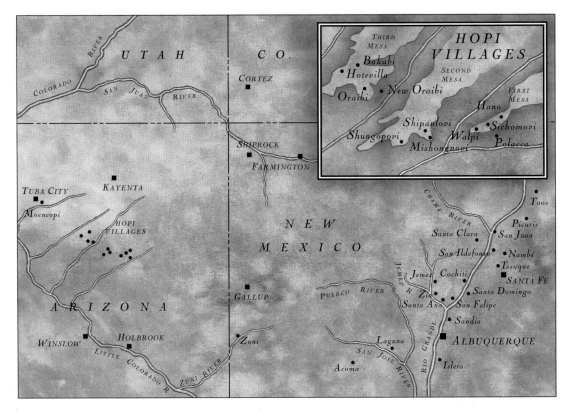

Jemez. To the west, on the sunset slope of the Continental Divide, is the pueblo of Zuni on the banks of the Zuni River. Far to the west in Arizona, occupying the three stony fingers of Black Mesa, are the eleven villages of the Shoshonean Hopi and a small settlement of Tewa people. Even farther west are the outlying Hopi villages of Upper and Lower Moencopi.

Some of these small towns are at greater elevations than others. Some lie along streams where irrigation is possible, while others are in arid lands where dry farming is the only option. Nonetheless, all are farmers, and their principal crop is corn.

Every village of these disparate people can have performances by at least one group of sacred clowns. If asked about the nature of these clowns and why they exist, most Pueblo people will maintain a strict silence, or give the stock answer that they are only for amusement. When Hopi are asked about the importance of the clowns, their actions, and their purpose, the explanation depends upon the age and position of the one who answers. The elders or chiefs justify clowning by saying, "They are worth something. They do it for rain, crops, fertility."[1] Others, somewhat younger and often more acculturated, will express a humanistic philosophy with the statement, "The clowns represent ourselves. They do all the things we do. They act like children. They don't know how to behave. They come down the ladders head-first and they make jokes. The

clowns always realize their bad behavior and confess it in a funny way and the crowd laughs. The kachinas do not take any notice of the clowns. The kachinas are always the same. They represent unchanging law—eternity."[2] When the youngest are asked they declare, "It is just to make the people laugh." Implicit in these statements is the understanding that the kachinas enjoy coming where the people are happy, and the clowns are the ultimate "Delight Makers."

However, in addition to amusement, another function is indicated by the preceding statements, the underlying drive to maintain cultural cohesion and preserve the status quo. To achieve this, any deviant behavior, whether that of strangers and their idiosyncrasies, or more importantly, problems within the village, is grist for the clowns' performance. All forms of humor are used, with mockery and caricature being the clowns' main method of ridiculing any trans-

The Kokopell' Mana is the female partner (played by a man) of the Hump-backed Flute Player Kachina. "She" appears with the Runner Kachinas and is passionately fond of men. If she can catch a man, she flings him to the ground and imitates copulation.

L. Dallas, Moencopi, year unknown. 7" Frank and Patricia Marie Collection.

gression of accepted social mores. As a consequence, there is an inordinate fear on the part of the individual of having one's shortcomings exposed to village scrutiny through the activities of the clowns. The fact that no one, regardless of age or station, is immune from these vignettes of ridicule further strengthens this aspect. The result is that the clown is the ultimate keeper of tradition.

In addition to the roles of entertainer and keeper of traditional ways, Pueblo clowns have, or have had, a number of other functions, including routing out the dancers, racers, and workers for

Four Tewa clowns or Koshari during a break in the Holi dance.

Courtesy of Anna Kopta and University of New Mexico Photo Archives

Right: He is commonly referred to as the Mocking Kachina but his name Kwikwilyaka, or Striped-Over, refers to his nose and eyes. Here he is attired in a gay nineties bathing suit, for some reason or other, with the skeleton of a fish in one hand and a pole in the other.

Daryl Seckletstewa, pueblo and year unknown. 12" E. Comins Collection.

pueblo projects; as hunt managers; and as scouts or warriors. On a more dangerous level they practice magic and help in the warding off of witches.[3] These roles differ depending upon the pueblo, the type of clown, and the amount of intertribal borrowing. While a matter of conjecture among cultural anthropologists, indications are that the sacred clown belongs both to the Underworld and the normal Upper World and possesses attributes of both.

For the Hopi, the Underworld is the antithesis of the normal world: when it is winter here it is summer there; whoever is ugly here is handsome there; here, beings are solid and unchangeable while there, the body is insubstantial and mutable. Every attribute is reversed, which may account for the clowns saying the opposite of what they mean, for their association with the dead, and for their coming over the clouds to the villages.

As inhabitants of both worlds, the clowns also become the caretakers, or "fathers," of the kachinas, able to announce their arrival, albeit in an obverse manner, care for their appearance as they dance, and serve as interpreters between the two worlds.

There is one element that separates the sacred clowns from all others who may act as clowns or buffoons. That is the rigidly pre-scribed scenario that they follow and around which they construct their humorous themes. These skits vary with the moment and may portray such things as trivial marital problems, critical land dis-putes with neighbors, or merely the strange activities of the domi-nant culture that surrounds them. All of their humor, however, is designed to ridicule unseemly actions and to bring about uniformity of behavior by presenting life as it should *not* be lived. Most common

are burlesques of the ordinary. A trifling occurrence is treated as a momentous event or the reverse, an exaggerated display of a common emotion, is portrayed, or distinctive characteristics of a visitor or a villager are caricatured.

Essentially, the clowns isolate the core of a current event and reduce it to the ridiculous. Both verbal and visual punning are greatly enjoyed, particularly when a double meaning can be used, often with a vulgar or obscene version that can be presented. Any form of humor that can be brought into play to produce laughter will be utilized, but it will always be within the parameters of the traditional scenario.

When the clowns paint themselves in unique ways before appearing, they are not merely adorning their bodies with haphazard decoration. They are putting on designs that invoke their patron and incorporate his personae. In the manner of a shaman, the clown becomes one with his patron and uses that being's powers to accomplish his ends. In the manner of a priest, the clown makes manifest the needs of both the Underworld and the villagers of the Upper World.

Inevitably, the importance of these sacred clowns produces a support organization that clusters about their performances. Such societies or cults teach and advise on the basis of past performances, initiate new members, and monitor current activities. As a society, it will have a chief or headman who has stewardship of the altars, fetishes, and other ritual paraphernalia unique to the cult. Such societies exist in the Rio Grande and, with the exception of the Hopi, in the western pueblos as well.

Among the Hopi, fragmentary evidence indicates that in earlier times such organizations existed, although this is no longer true. On First Mesa, the Hopi Clown Society ceased in the early years of the nineteenth century,[4] and that of the adjoining Tewa, by the end of the same century.[5] On Third Mesa, the Eagle Clan maintains that it alone is the owner of the Paiyatamu clowns, yet they have no chief, altar, or ritual gear, and have not been active for many years.[6] Despite the loss of supporting organizations, the clowns continue to perform in every village.

The Hopi have four groups of clowns:[7] the Tsukuwimkya, the Paiyakyamu or Kossa, the Koyemsi, and the Piptuyakyamu. Two are native to the Hopi: the formal Tsukuwimkya, the sacred clowns, and the informal buffoons, the Piptuyakyamu. The presence of the other two reflects both the Pueblo ethic of borrowing and the Hopi propensity for elaboration. Accidents of history have brought the Koyemsi as a relatively recent import from Zuni to be fused with an

Left: The Kwikwilyaka or Mocking Kachina is frequently mentioned as a clown. However, it is not one of the sacred clowns but is instead a kachina whose actions are inherently amusing; he imitates anyone who is near him, despite their desperate efforts to get rid of him.

Ronald Honyouti, Bakavi, year unknown. 6" Frank and Patricia Marie Collection.

Koyemsi at play in a puddle of rain water in Oraibi during a Chakwaina dance.

Courtesy of John Wilson

Right: The Huhuwa or Cross-Legged Kachina represents a man who presumably once lived at Mishongnovi. This individual was always happy, so kind and helpful to the people despite his disability that it is believed when he died he became a kachina who behaves as did the man. Dolls made of this individual are usually humorous in appearance.

(left) Wilfred Tewawina, Moencopi, 1987. 5" S. Simpson Collection. (right) Wilfred Tewawina, Moencopi, year unknown. 11" J. Bialac Collection.

indigenous form, the Tachukti.[8] The Paiyakyamu, an introduction from the eastern pueblos, probably came with the immigrant Tewa people and are usually known by the name of the Kossa or Koshari.[9] Both the Tsukuwimkya and the Paiyakyamu are sacred clowns, while the Piptuyakyamu would be considered secular.[10] The Koyemsi represent a different class of beings for whom clowning is but one of several roles. Each of these groups is further divided by recognizable variations in color, costume, and attributes. Although some of these differences may appear to be insignificant to the casual observer, they identify distinct individuals easily recognized by the Hopi.

Identification of these groups and their subdivisions is often rendered difficult by the inclusiveness of many of their names, particularly those used in early ethnographic records. For instance, the term "Paiyakyamu" is the name used for the Kossa (both the Koshari and the Kwirena). It is also used specifically for the Koshari and, in addition, it is occasionally applied to all Hopi clowns,[11] which would include the Tsukuwimkya and the Tachukti.

Delineation of Hopi clowns is made more difficult by the fact that there are kachinas (both important and not so important) whose actions may be likened to those of a clown, who behave in a clownish manner, or who are capable of producing situations that are inherently funny, but who cannot be considered as clowns. A partial listing of these is included.

Another group that is nebulous but has been mentioned among Hopi people is one of masked beings who are considered to be clowns only for the kachinas. No attempt has been made to separate this category.

CLOWNS AND KOYEMSI

Tsukuwimkyamu[12] *(Unmasked)*

A. Sikya Tsutskutu,[13] The Yellow Clowns
- Sikya Tsuku — Yellow Clown
- Paiyatam' — Red-Striped Yellow Clown
  (Men of the Wuwuchim and Tataukyamu societies
  are informal members of this clown group.)[14]

B. Ko-Tsutskutu, The White Clowns
- Köcha Tsuku — White Clown
- Na'somta Tsuku — Hair Knot Clown[15]

C. O-Tsutskutu — The Red Clowns[16]

Paiyakyamu[17] *(Unmasked)*

A. Koshari or Koyala — The Hano Clown
- Sakwa Koshari — Blue Hano Clown
- Sikya Koshari — Yellow Hano Clown
- Kuwan Koshari — Colorful Hano Clown

B. Kwirena or Kaisale — The Single-Horned Clown

C. Kaisale Mana (Mana is "girl")

Paiyatamu (Spirit)

Koyemsi (Masked)

A. Tachukti — Ball-on-Head[18]

B. Koyemsi — Mudhead
- Kuikuinaka Koyemsi — Starter Mudhead
- Powamu Koyemsi — Bean Dance Mudhead
- Kipok Koyemsi — Warrior Mudhead
- Toson Koyemsi — Sweet-Cornmeal-Tasting Mudhead
- Powak Koyemsi — Witch Mudhead
- Tuvé Koyemsi — Replacement Mudhead
- Mongwi Koyemsi — Chief Mudhead, Bragger
- Pushun' Koyemsi — Drummer Mudhead
- Koyemsi'kima — Mudhead Carrying
- Hishot Koyemsi — Ancient Mud Head
- Tatatsimu Koyemsi — Ball Player Mudheads

C. Koyemsihoya — Mudhead puppet

D. Koyemsi Mana — Mudhead Girl

Piptuyakyamu (*Masked and Unmasked*)

The Piptuyakyamu come in any guise they choose and, consequently, are of almost infinite variety. They are usually white-faced and unmasked but if the role demands it, they will appear in ad hoc masks. Despite the changeable nature of their appearance, several have assumed distinct identities and are no longer ephemeral. Characteristic of this latter type are the following:

A. Tasavu — Navajo Clown
B. Köcha Omau-u Tsuku — White Cloud Clown[19]
C. Si-chaiz Tsuku — Yellow Cloud Clown[20]

COMIC KACHINAS

A. Choqapölö — Mud Thrower
B. Choshuhuwa — Bluebird Snare Kachina
C. Heheya Aumutaka — Ladies' Man
D. Ho-e *or* Wo-e
E. Huhuwa — Cross-Legged Kachina
F. Kokopelli — Hump-Backed Kachina
G. Kokopell' Mana — Hump-Backed Kachina Girl
H. Kwikwilyaka — Mocking Kachina
I. Mastop — Death Fly Kachina
J. Qöqöle
K. Sakwats Mana — Worming Girl
L. Tasaf Yeibichai — Navajo Grandfather

KACHINAS WHO PRODUCE COMIC SITUATIONS

A. Atosle — an Ogre Kachina
B. Chaveyo — an Ogre Kachina
C. Chilikomato — Chili Pepper Kachina
D. Hahai-i Wuhti — Pour-Water-Woman
E. Masau-u — Deity of the Underworld
F. Momo — Bee Kachina
G. Pachok'china — Cocklebur Kachina
H. Soyok' Wuhti — Ogre Woman
I. Ushé — Hano Cactus Kachina
J. Wik'china — Greasy One
K. Yoche — Apache Kachina
L. Yohozro Wuhti — Cold-Bringing Woman

2

THE TSUKUWIMKYA

Above: Two Tsutskutu in full dress at Oraibi.
Courtesy of Bethel College

Left: The first of these Red-Striped or Paiyatum' Clowns is a weight lifter with a bad piece of equipment. The next two are trying to get the watermelon the top one has already taken from the pole. The fifth, carrying a water-melon, has red earrings of dyed rabbit fur. The last clown appears to have sore hands from using his hoe.

(left) Tyson Namoki, pueblo unknown, 1990. 8" S. Simpson Collection. (pole) Vincent Dawahongva, pueblo and year unknown. 28" J. Bialac Collection. (third right) Ronald Honahnie, pueblo unknown, 1992. 9" S. Simpson Collection. (right) Baldwin Huma, pueblo and year unknown. 7" E. Comins Collection.

THE TSUKUWIMKYA ARE THE SACRED CLOWNS OF THE HOPI and follow a traditionally prescribed unchanging routine. They appear only in the afternoon during the spring and summer plaza dances. Although there are several subdivisions within this group, their paraphernalia is basically the same: a kerchief of old cloth about the neck, black yarn at the wrists and knees, and a breechclout, or nowadays a pair of shorts. A piece of cloth is wrapped around the waist over the top of these. Each clown has a small bag of cornmeal hanging around his neck, and looped across his torso from the right shoulder to the left waist is a thin bandoleer made of strips of yucca to which is tied a piece of piki bread and a bit of spruce—"journey food."[1] Any old, decrepit, or mismatched pair of shoes or moccasins is worn on his feet, and usually a few hoofs or horns are attached to one leg as a rattle.

Because of the belief that the clowns are coming from the clouds,[2] their entry into the village is always across the roof tops. Here they make their way, stepping on or over any obstacles or on-lookers on the roof tops and behaving like ignorant, rude children until they reach a rooftop above the plaza. Upon arriving, they crawl to the edge and peer down into the plaza. They spring to

Fig. 2.
*Sikya Na'somta
Tsuku*

Fig. 1.
Sikya Tsuku

their feet with stentorian yells, throwing their arms wide and subsiding only to repeat this action, usually four times. Having announced their presence, they begin to gabble and argue among themselves. The gist of this noisy diatribe is to suggest that they are on a mountain top and have just perceived activity in a valley far below them. They are trying to decide whether, and how, they are going to go down and see what the activity is all about.

Because it is supposed to be a long and difficult trip, the clowns enter the plaza from the roof tops in the most ill-conceived, inefficient, awkward, mirth-provoking method they can devise.[3] Head first down a ladder and falling in a heap at the bottom, or lowered clinging to the end of a long pole or swung inside a tire at the end of a length of rope, invariably they end up in a heap on the plaza floor amid loud exclamations and protests.

Once there, they seem for a time to be completely oblivious to the kachinas dancing alongside them. Suddenly, they discover the kachinas and set about trying to find out what they are. They pull and poke, yell remarks, and even drag a kachina out of the dance line to shout questions at him as though he were deaf.

The kachinas, of course, never speak and submit gracefully to this rude treatment. Receiving no answers, the clowns continue on around the line until they chance upon the kachina father, the village representative who leads the kachinas in and out of the plaza.

Fig. 3.
Sikya Tsuku

Fig. 4.
Sikya Tsuku

This man explains who the kachinas are and how they bring the blessings of good crops, rain, fertility, and health to the Hopi from the deities. With that information, each of the clowns rushes wildly about trying to claim all of the kachinas for himself by running around the kachina line with arms outstretched to indicate all that are his. This provokes a great deal of loud arguing among the clowns.

Slowly, the realization comes to them that they do not know how to get these benefits from the kachinas, and they dash back to the kachina father for instructions. After he patiently explains how the Hopi send their prayers with the kachinas, the clowns immediately set about trying to find the leader of the kachinas so they can offer their prayers. After much searching, they discover the leader because he is the only one who will answer by shaking his rattle. After he is found, the clowns take turns loudly stating their thoughtless wants to him. Greedily they ask for all the wrong things, such as "mountains of corn," "good-looking girls," "a Cadillac," etc., and, taking prayermeal from the bags around their necks, they fling it wildly at the kachinas. As each clown finishes his prayer, the kachina leader shakes his rattle to signify that he understands.

When the kachina dancers finish their set and leave for the rest area, the clowns discover a small spruce tree planted at one end of

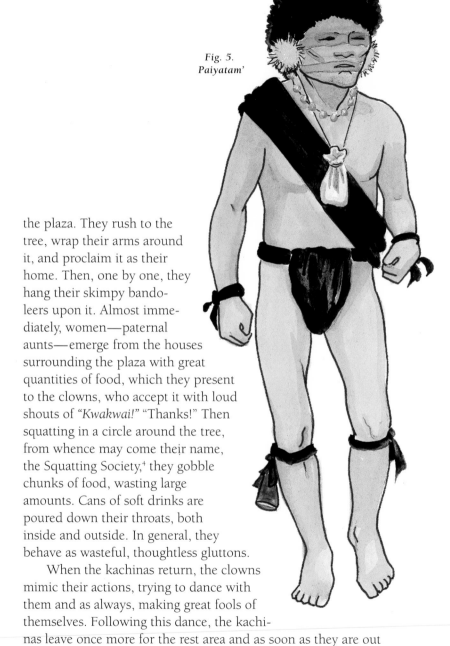

Fig. 5.
Paiyatam'

the plaza. They rush to the tree, wrap their arms around it, and proclaim it as their home. Then, one by one, they hang their skimpy bando-leers upon it. Almost imme-diately, women—paternal aunts—emerge from the houses surrounding the plaza with great quantities of food, which they present to the clowns, who accept it with loud shouts of *"Kwakwai!"* "Thanks!" Then squatting in a circle around the tree, from whence may come their name, the Squatting Society,[4] they gobble chunks of food, wasting large amounts. Cans of soft drinks are poured down their throats, both inside and outside. In general, they behave as wasteful, thoughtless gluttons.

When the kachinas return, the clowns mimic their actions, trying to dance with them and as always, making great fools of themselves. Following this dance, the kachi-nas leave once more for the rest area and as soon as they are out of the plaza, the clowns decide to build a house for themselves and install their "sister" in it to take care of them. This sister, or girl, is

Four Tsutskutu at play in the Oraibi plaza. At the right a Tasap Yeibichai urges them onward. In the left background is a Piptu Wuhti with a hoe.

Courtesy of Bethel College

usually an old, ratty, stuffed water bird or a rag doll stuck in the back of the leader's breechclout. This self-appointed "boss" tells the other clowns what they will need in the way of supplies to build their house. Suggestions fly, and one clown will ask for "French doors," another for "picture windows," or "a stair case," "a Jacuzzi," or whatever other incongruous thing the clowns can think of installing. The leader then sends them off to get these items. They return almost immediately, not with anything constructive, but with handfuls of ashes and charcoal with which they mark the outline of their "house" on the plaza floor. Often they make believe that they have locked themselves in or out of this ash outline.

After installing their "girl" in their home to take care of them, and wasting some more food, they continue with the clowning routine they have chosen. They may run races or play games with each other, with the children in the audience, or with some exotically dressed outsider. Their antics will include making fun of any current problem, event, personality, tribal visitor, or whatever they deem appropriate to mock or ridicule. The clowns poke fun at anything and everyone. Their conduct becomes more and more outrageous until at last, the Warrior Kachinas appear to threaten them. These punitive kachinas usually come on the second day of the dance and include beings such as the Great Horned Owl, Crow, Chosbusi Kachina, or Kipok Koyemsi.

Fig. 6. Paiyatamhoya (1900)

17

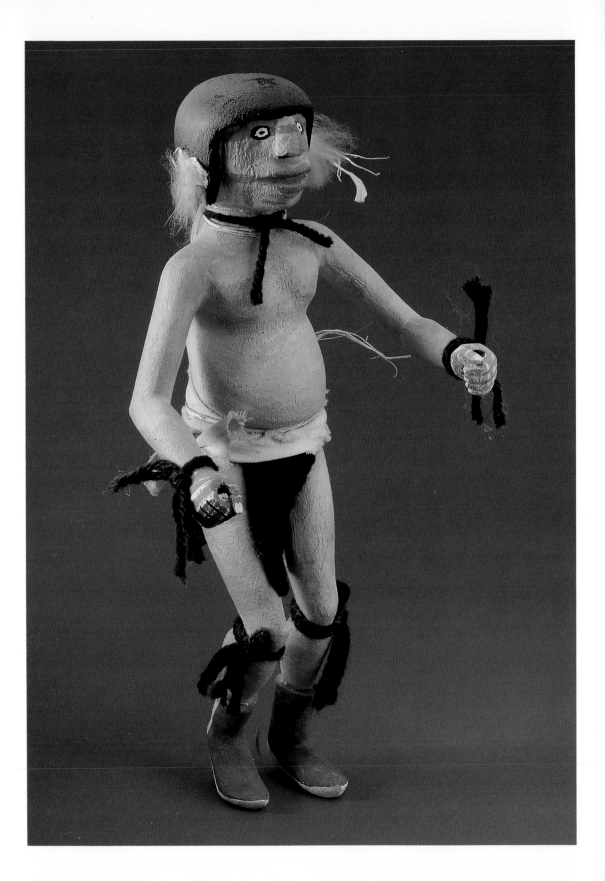

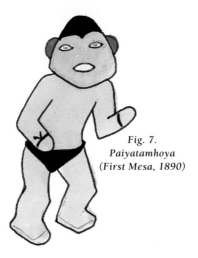

Fig. 7.
Paiyatamhoya
(First Mesa, 1890)

Fig. 8.
Paiyatamhoya
(Oraibi, 1960)

One of these kachinas will appear for a moment at an entrance where his presence will be noted by the clowns. After a momentary start at this apparition, they make scoffing remarks and then ignore him. The kachina disappears but returns shortly, often with another warrior who will appear at a different entrance. This time the first kachina enters the plaza and talks to the "boss" clown before leaving once more. Although the leader promises to do better, the clowns continue on as heedlessly as before while more of the warriors appear to threaten them. On their fourth and last appearance, the Warrior Kachinas attack the clowns without mercy, thrashing them with willow switches, stripping them of their breechclouts or shorts, piling them in a heap, and committing other indignities before drenching them with water.

The clowns plead for forgiveness and one by one, in acts of "atonement," they "confess" to the most outrageous events, usually sexual in content, and occasionally involving a relative. As each clown begins his story, he does a little sidewise hop to punctuate his tale. At the end of this episode, the clowns assemble in complete seriousness to sprinkle cornmeal on the kachinas in proper fashion before retiring to the kiva with them, thus ending their performance.

This format is followed by all of the Yellow, Red-Striped Yellow, and White Clowns. The Koshari follow the same routine, but neither the Koyemsi nor the Piptuka ever engage in this ritual.

Left: A Red-Striped Clown readies himself for some sort of action as he has put aside his little bandoleer and meal pouch.
Carver unknown, pueblo and year unknown. 8" J. Jacka Collection.

SIKYA TSUTSKUTU, YELLOW CLOWNS

Sikya Tsuku, Yellow Clown

Although he can appear in any village, the Sikya Tsuku, or Yellow Clown, is most frequently seen at Shungopovi and on fewer occasions at Third Mesa. The other Second Mesa villages of Shipaulovi and Mishongnovi seemingly prefer the Red-Striped Clown, their version of Paiyatamu, while First Mesa most consistently presents the White Clowns.

The Sikya Tsutskutu (figs. 1–4) pull their hair up into clumps, one at either side of the head and sometimes one on the front. They daub a thick yellow paint over their entire bodies and heads. Below their mouth and each eye, they paint thin arcs of black with the ends upturned. A black dot is placed under the nose and over each eye at eyebrow level. This decoration diverts the eye from the normal visage and renders the individual portraying the clown almost unidentifiable. They wear a piece of white cloth or blanket around their hips, particularly the "boss" clown, who uses it to hold the doll or bird that represents his "sister." In recent years, the traditional black breechclout has been abandoned for gaudy gym shorts with a short black kilt worn over the front of them. Tennis shoes, jogging shoes, cowboy boots, and even thongs may replace the brown moccasins in many instances.

Paiyatam', The Red-Striped Clowns

The Red-Striped Clown has a number of variations in appearance depending upon location, time, and other factors but it and the Sikya Tsutskutu are considered to be the only true Hopi clowns.[5] Typically, this clown appears with face and body painted yellow. When the red stripes (sutangaroki) or Konin marks (a reference to the source of the red paint), are present on the Sikya Tsuku, the clown is called Paiyatam' and considered to be different.[6] Across the eyes, from ear to ear, is a reddish-brown line, while another red line crosses the mouth from one angle of the jaw to the other (figs. 5–6). Otherwise both are referred to as the Sikya Tsutskut (figs. 7–8) even though the hair style is different.

The head of the clown is covered with a black sheepskin wig, the wool cut to a short length. Red-stained tufts of rabbit fur are used for earrings. In addition, he wears a necklace that may be either tufts of red-stained rabbit fur or, more usually, the striped yellow-and-white fruit of the deadly nightshade. He also carries a small bag of prayer meal around his neck. A woman's black cape

Two Hopi Yellow Clowns (Sikya Tsutskutu). The one in the foreground is holding a roll of red piki bread in his hand and has a look of anticipation on his face. The one in the background is a caricature of someone cooking, wearing a straw hat.

Wilfred Tewawina, Moencopi, 1960–1970. 16"
Margaret Kilgore Collection.

(*ushimni*) is rolled and slung over the right shoulder then brought down to the left hip and attached. This item is the only variation in dress from that of the Sikya Tsutskutu.

The Red-Striped Clown is called Paiyatamhoya, or less often, Paiyatam', on Second Mesa (a puppet form is also called Paiyatamhoya), while on Third Mesa, the clowns are the Paiyatamu. The Second Mesa Paiyatamhoya is dressed and colored in an identical fashion to the other Red-Striped Clowns, except that the painting of the face differs. Both the eyes and mouth are represented by white half-circles with black centers rising above horizontal red lines (figs. 9–11). This style of painting the eyes is similar to other

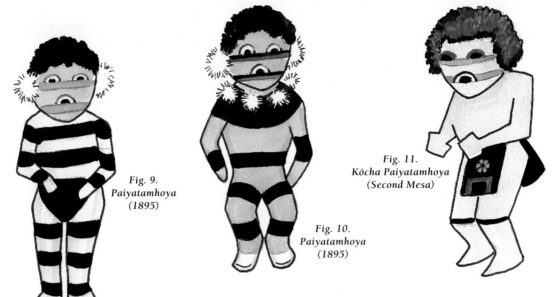

Fig. 9.
Paiyatamhoya
(1895)

Fig. 11.
Köcha Paiyatamhoya
(Second Mesa)

Fig. 10.
Paiyatamhoya
(1895)

symbolic renditions of the sun rising over the eastern horizon as seen in the mark for the Sun's Forehead Clan, Omau-u Humikumi Kachina, and others. While it may not be so in this instance, it does take on more importance considering that Paiyatamu or Taiowa, the patron of the clowns, is supposed to be the son of the Sun and to reside on the eastern horizon.

Paiyatam' makes an appearance on First Mesa also, although the preference there is for the Köcha Tsutskutu. Despite this preference, when the First Mesa Clown Dance is given, the face painting of both the males and the females more closely resembles that of the Red-Striped Clown (figs. 12–14).

Occasionally, the bodies of dolls, or *tihu*, of Paiyatamhoya, particularly in early collections, are striped with black horizontal bands on both the yellow and white forms in the manner of the Koshari. There is a Paiyatam' with a white body (figs. 11 and 15) as well as a version painted in a number of colors, the Kuwan Paiyatam' (fig. 16). Little is known concerning the Kuwan Paiyatam' except that he is present in some of the collections of older kachina dolls and often comes as a drummer. The Paiyatam' are also made into the flat dolls that are given to young children (figs. 17–18).

When the Paiyatam' come to the villages, they follow the same traditional scenario as the Sikya Tsutskutu, with one exception. Because members of the Tataokyamu and Wuwuchimtu men's societies are considered to be informal clowns, they may volunteer to clown for the kachinas as Paiyatamu. As such, they are indistinguishable from the other Paiyatam'. However, in one kind of performance, groups of them may come and direct all of their ribald

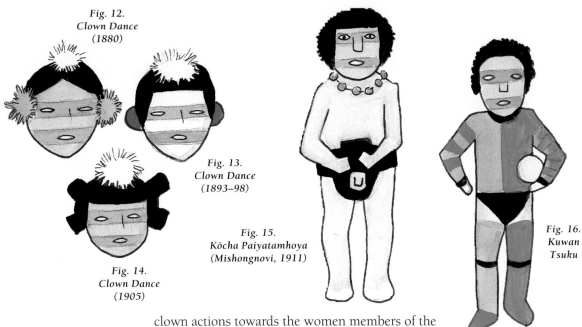

Fig. 12.
Clown Dance
(1880)

Fig. 13.
Clown Dance
(1893–98)

Fig. 14.
Clown Dance
(1905)

Fig. 15.
Kŏcha Paiyatamhoya
(Mishongnovi, 1911)

Fig. 16.
Kuwan
Tsuku

clown actions towards the women members of the
Mamzrau society. They sing obscene songs about
them and make all manner of jeering remarks about the women,
who retaliate by dumping vile water on them.[7] For this appearance
the men dress as the usual Paiyatam' except for their hair. Instead of
being covered with a sheepskin wig, the hair is all gathered together
and mixed with split cornhusks, then twisted into a hornlike pro-
jection on the top of the head (fig. 19). This is the same style as the
informal clowns, the Nepaiyatemu (fig. 20) of Zuni.[8] The Zuni
clown chief (fig. 21) also resembles the Hopi Wuwuchim. The two
faces are almost identical.

There is a small wooden puppet of Paiyatamu that is called
Tsukuhoya or Paiyatamhoya, this latter term is a duplication of
the name for the Second Mesa Red-Striped Clown. The puppet is thought to have a life of its own and consequently is
considered more like a kachina than a clown.

Another form with a similar name should
also be mentioned. On Third Mesa there was
formerly a Paiyata-um Kachina as well.[9] At
the Hopi pueblo of Old Oraibi on Third
Mesa, it was known as the Paiyata-um
Kachina (fig. 22) and resembled a Second
Mesa Paiyatamhoya with Koshari horns. It
came with a plaza dance group resembling
the Palhik' Mana, a corn performance at
Old Oraibi,[10] where it reputedly danced at
the front of the line as the leader. Despite

Fig. 17.
Flat doll,
Clown Dance

Fig. 18.
Flat doll,
Clown Dance

Fig. 19.
Hopi Wuwuchim

Fig. 20.
Zuni Nepaiyatemu

Fig. 21.
Zuni Clown Chief

the fact that the face and body are painted like the Paiyatamhoya clown of Second Mesa and it wears black-and-white horns like the Koshari, the Paiyata-um Kachina is dressed in full kachina garb, wears a mask, and behaves as a kachina and not a clown.

Lange states that at Cochiti a Ku'shali (Koshari) clown leads a Pai'yat-yama Kachina into the plaza. However, this kachina most closely resembles the Kaisale of the Hopi in its multicolored markings. The Cochiti version comes as a motion-maker in the Frijoles Canyon Dance (*Dyu'weni*), a springtime Corn Dance.[11]

KÖCHA TUTSKUTU, THE WHITE CLOWNS

Na'somta Tsuku

There are two variations of white clowns: the Hair-knot Clown, *Na'somta Tsuku* (fig. 23), by far the most common, and the ordinary white clown, *Köcha Tsuku* (fig. 24). These clowns paint themselves all white with a limy clay that occurs along the mesa edge below the cliff-forming Mesa Verde formation. When the clay dries on their bodies, it leaves them splotched white.

The Na'somta Tsutskutu (Hair-Knot Clowns) differ in headdress from the ordinary White Clowns. They divide their hair into two queues, one on either side of the head in the manner of the maiden's hair knots, rather than into the little pigtails or clumps of hair and cornhusk present on the Sikya Tsuku. The two queues are held upright by a string that ties them together across the back of the head. Around their hips they wear a rolled-up black blanket or

Fig. 22.
Paiyata-um Kachina

Fig. 23.
Na'somta Tsuku

Fig. 24.
O-oto Tsuku

woman's cape, while the remainder of their costume is like that
of the Yellow Clowns. Occasionally this clown will be painted all
yellow just like the Sikya Tsutskutu except for the presence of the
small hair knots (fig. 2). This may be an aberration rather than a
true variation.

A version of the Na'somta Tsutskutu differs in that they tie
stuffed ground squirrels or prairie dogs to long strings and throw
them at the kachinas to frighten them.[12] They often have a black
spot on either cheek and wear a double black yarn bandoleer
(fig. 24). One Hopi man called this clown O-oto Tsuku, or Ground
Squirrel Clown.

Köcha Tsuku

The ordinary Köcha Tsutskutu (White Clowns) are identical with
the Sikya Tsutskutu, or Yellow Clowns, except that they paint their
bodies white instead of yellow and do not use the black dots above
the eyes and mouth and paint their faces in the manner of the
Koshari.

At Zuni two homologues for the White Clowns belong to the
Galaxy Society. They are the Newekwe (fig. 25) and the Hewa Hewa
buffoon (fig. 26). Parsons considered them to be homologues for
the Koshari and in this she was undoubtedly correct, but they also
correspond to the Hopi Tsutskutu. The roles of both of these
clowns are closely related to that of the Newekwe, as are some of
their visual characteristics. They first paint their heads and bodies
with a gray clay taken from their sacred spring, *Lutkyanakwe,* or

The Kōcha Tsuku on the left has apparently just graduated and is going to the 1978 All-Indian Pow Wow with a bag of money around his neck and all of his toilet articles in another bag in his left hand. He is ready for the world! The other clown (right) is into physical fitness and is jumping rope. (left) Henry Shelton, Oraibi, 1978. 10" E. Comins Collection. (right) Keith Torres, pueblo and year unknown. 11" E. Comins Collection.

Fig. 25.
Zuni Newekwe

Fig. 26.
Zuni Hewa Hewa

Ash Spring,[13] and put an arc of black under each eye. Their mouth decoration varies in that the Newekwe paint the arc with the points downward and the Hewa Hewa paint an enclosing red line around the mouth and use a dot over each eye.

The Hopi clowns, whether using white or yellow clay, do not seem to take it from a spring or sacred area but mark their faces in much the same fashion. All of them cover their heads, some by wrapping a cloth around to make a tight skull cap, or by pulling the hair tightly against the skull, leaving two tufts of hair at either side of the head. The Hopi usually mix corn husks with the hair tufts, while the Zuni make the tufts entirely of corn husks. The Hopi make a third tuft on the forehead and the Zuni at the back of the head.

O-TSUTSKUTU

The Red Clowns described by Stephen were called O-Tsutskutu[14] by some of the older Hopi, who said that they were no longer seen. During Stephen's time, they had neither altar nor chief and so there could be no formal initiation. At that time, however, when individuals were initiated as Tsukuwimkya, they were not painted yellow or white but were instead smeared with red ochre over their heads and bodies. Their hair was pulled up into bunches on the sides of their heads and the usual black arcs were put under the mouth and eyes with black dots above (fig. 27). This was done without regard for the age or sex of the individual. It was considered an informal

Fig. 27.
Palatsutskutu
(male)

Fig. 28.
Palatsutskutu
(female)

initiation but nevertheless made the individuals true Tsukuwimkya members.

In the case of the Tsuku Wuhti (fig. 28), the woman was smeared with red only over the head and shoulders, and her dress was never removed. Her hair was taken down and retied in bunches at either side of the head, then smeared with red. The mouth was marked differently from the male Tsuku in that a black line was drawn from the arc below the mouth to the center of the lower lip, making the Hopi symbol for a vulva. It is not known whether the Tsuku Wuhti were formerly a regular part of a clown society, were specific individuals similar to the initiates, or were selected at random.[15] Whether this was only an occasional representation or not is unknown.

In their actions, the Red Clowns behaved in the same manner as all clowns, even the women, who were mature individuals. Regardless, the initiates, or Red Clowns, seem to have ceased to be presented by the turn of the century. At least no record or remembrance of them exists after the 1890s. It is possible that they were a part of clown society that fell into disuse during this period.

The following episodes are typical of the actions of the clowns. During the late 1960s, there was a flare-up in the sightings of flying saucers, which the clowns put to good use in the plaza at Shungopovi on Second Mesa. The clowns were busily racing with the children when an eerie sound was heard. It resembled the noise of an object traveling at high speed through the atmosphere. As it came nearer, the clowns panicked, running about, babbling, and generally creating confusion. Then two bright, shining saucers sailed from behind the houses on one side of the plaza and disappeared over the houses on the other side, which produced even greater consternation among the clowns.

Nothing further happened and the great hullabaloo slowly diminished, only to be suddenly revived as over the rooftops came green men dressed in silvery clothing. They demanded that the clowns take them to their leader. After great fear at first, the clowns then forgot all about their visitors as they fell into an argument as to who was their leader.

The effects had been created by whirling a piece of hose around to produce the noise, gluing two pie pans together and weighting them so they could be easily thrown, and painting some individuals green and making their clothing of aluminum foil. The entire episode was a burlesque of a leader at a nearby village who was making a great public uproar over flying saucers.

Another timely performance occurred during a tribal council election year. The Hopi were inundated with political speeches and promises designed to get various individuals elected. As a result, the clowns felt obligated to campaign as well. One afternoon, a solemn procession of clowns dressed as politicians came striding into the plaza, moving with obvious self-importance. Each was well-dressed in a shirt and fancy tie, with suit coat carefully buttoned in place, but unfortunately none of the clowns was wearing pants. The sight of bare yellow legs protruding below their suit jackets was convulsively funny. Carrying briefcases stuffed with countless papers, they took turns mounting a large box, where each presented his platform and programs amid great roars of laughter.

In yet another instance, the clowns succeeded in finding some clothing of extra-large dimensions. Some blue denims were large enough for two clowns to fit inside, one in each leg. Others were great shirts and overalls which the clowns proceeded to stuff with odds and ends. The plaza appeared to be crowded with numbers of hugely fat people. Unable to walk easily, these beings waddled about and occasionally fell over and were unable to get to their feet without help. Two attempted to dance together but could not reach one another over the immensity of their bodies. Although the episode was quite short, the actions of the clowns in doing ordinary things produced hysterical laughter from the audience. The message presented by the clowns was clear and the laughing audience needed no interpretation.

THE HOPI CLOWNS (Tsutskutu)
The large central figure is a generalized Yellow Clown (Sikya Tsuku) based on a variety of sources. The other two Yellow Clowns, to the right of the central figure, are individual interpretations of the same clown. The Red Clowns (Palatsutskutu) at upper left are the male (top) and female clown initiates. The Hairknot Clowns (Na'somta Tsutsukutu) below the Red Clowns, named for their hairdress, may come in either white (O-oto) or yellow. The two heads at upper right show similar clown figures at Zuni, the Newekwe (left) and the Hewa Hewa.

THE HOPI RED-STRIPED CLOWNS (Paiyatam')
The large central figure is a generalized Red-Striped Clown based on a number of sources. Counterclockwise from upper left, individual interpretations are from First Mesa in 1890, from 1890, and from Oraibi in 1960; occasionally this clown comes with a white body, as shown in two examples; a Clown Dance is given on First Mesa, as shown with the three heads at lower right, and flat dolls are made of it, as shown in the two figures above the heads; there are also minor variations like the green-and-red figure, Kuwan Paiyatam', and the Second Mesa types shown to the right of it; Zuni figures like the Nepaiyatemu at upper right and the Clown Chief to the left of it resemble the Hopi Wuwuchim (top center) in style of headdress.

This kachina is called either Ho-e or Wo-e; there is no English word for either name. He is a clownish figure that comes with the kachinas during the late winter Powamu ceremony. His humorous behavior is that of an irresponsible but lovable clown who accompanies the reserved Chief Kachinas as well as the fierce guards and warrior kachinas. (left) Delbridge Honahnie, Shungopovi, year unknown. 10" J. Bialac Collection. (right) Clifford Lomaheftewa, Shungopovi, 1986. 12" S. Simpson Collection.

THE PAIYAKYAMU OR KOSSA

THE KOSHARI IS PROBABLY ONE OF THE BEST-KNOWN FIGURES and the most frequently carved clowns on the Hopi mesas. His appearance is so well known that many believe that the Koshari and the Koyemsi are the only Hopi clowns. Yet the Koyemsi is not a clown and the Koshari is of Tewa, not Hopi, origin.

Undoubtedly, the Koshari arrived with the Tewa immigrants from the northern end of the Rio Grande valley in the early eighteenth century.[1] He has been so thoroughly assimilated that now he may be found on all three of the Hopi Mesas. However, the Koshari is just one-half of a clown pair known as the Kossa. This term, *Kossa*, is used to refer to both the Kwirena, or Winter Clowns, and the Koshari, or Summer Clowns.

As sacred clowns, the Kossa are the fathers of the kachinas,[2] the purveyors of village mores, and the keepers of tradition, just as are the Hopi Tsukuwimkya. Although their avowed purpose is to amuse,[3] the direction their humor takes is, as usual, concerned with that which is beyond the accepted Hopi way of life, be it outsiders, neighboring tribes, individuals, or attitudes that seem aberrant to the group.

The presence of the Kossa is constant throughout the Rio Grande pueblos as well as those to the west. While they may not have originated among the northern Tewa, this is a good starting point in considering their distribution. In the eastern pueblos, the Koshari and Kwirena societies and their patron Paiyatamu are reflections of a moiety social system, wherein the village is divided into balanced halves. One half is generally referred to as Winter People with their own kiva and the Kwirena clown society. The other, the Summer People, who have a different kiva, have the Koshari.

As one moves toward the western pueblos, moieties are replaced by clans (extended families descended from a common ancestor). This shift in the social system is reflected in the two clown groups. The Northern Tewa of New Mexico have a clearly defined moiety system and the two clown societies are associated with them. Their origin stories relate who the Kossa are and what their purpose is, as well as describing their appearance. This is one end of the spectrum. At the other end are the Hopi, where origin stories regarding the clowns are minimal.

Fig. 29.
Koshari

Traveling down the Rio Grande, both the Koshari and the Kwirena are found at Santa Ana and Santo Domingo,[4] and at San Felipe as the Koshare and the Quirena.[5] The equivalents of the Koshari are the Black Eyes of Isleta and the Ts'un'tabo'sh of Jemez.[6] At Cochiti, the Kossa are the Ku'shali (Koshari), a curing society, and the Kurena (Kwirena). The two societies are mutually exclusive and are closely tied to two others, Ku'shali with the Flint or *Hystiani,* a curing society and the Kurena with the *Cikame,* a hunting society.[7] Together, the Ku'shali and the Kurena manage almost every activity within the pueblo.[8]

At Acoma and Laguna, the Koshari are called the K'shale, presumably the same society as at Cochiti, and are still recognized as the equivalent of the Rio Grande Koshari. However, the Kwirena appears to have been lost in these pueblos.[9] At Zuni, the Koshare are identified as the Newekwe,[10] with "Kaishali," their alternate name, undoubtedly derived from the Cochiti usage as well.[11] There is almost no evidence of the Kwirena at Zuni.

At Hopi, where the Tewa immigrants exerted a strong influence, the two kinds of clowns re-emerge, but in asymmetrical form. The Koshari are present, easily recognizable as the eastern pueblo clowns. They are called the same name and retained bits of their societies' ceremonial structure until at least the turn of the century. The Kwirena are diminished and represented only by their clowns, the Kaisale, who are thought of as clowns for the kachinas.

At the Tewa village of Hano and the Hopi towns, each of the above terms seems to have been used. While the name Paiyakyamu was formerly used for all the clowns as well, the name was applied by the Hopi specifically to the black-and-white horned clowns. This term, Paiyakyamu, is recognized as a Tewa word and may be derived from Paiyatamu, the patron of these clowns. However, the derivation might be a little more complicated than this. *Kyamu* is a Hopi term that relates to the language of the Underworld, and is considered to be from the Keresans. It is also applied to the members of a society.[12]

KOSHARI, THE HANO CLOWN

The Kossa as a Hopi society became extinct in the late nineteenth century,[13] and the Kwirena virtually disappeared, a pattern common among the western pueblos. In modern times, these clowns are most frequently referred to by the Hopi as the Koshari (fig. 29) or Kaisale after the Keresan society to which they belonged. Another name for them is Koyala,[14] which seems to refer to their babbling speech and antic movements,[15] but may also relate to their headgear, *koya'lashen.*[16]

At First Mesa, Fewkes called the figures the Hano Gluttons because of their actions in the plaza and called them Tcukuwimkya as well.[17] In his publication, *Hopi Kachinas*, a Koshari is shown alongside a Kaisale Mana at the bottom of plate LVIII and is called by his other name, Paiakyamu, and also in the text, Hano Glutton. The drawing of the personage usually called Kaisale is at the top of

Fig. 30.
Sakwa
Koshari

Fig. 31.
Sikya
Koshari

Fig. 32.
Kuwan
Koshari

Fig. 33.
Koshari
Drummer

Left: The Hano Clown on a goat engaged in typical "play." He is enticing the animal to move by holding a stick with grass tied to the end of it. He is being "a cowboy" by riding, wearing cowboy boots, and waving a revolver. The maker is unknown but the style of carving is quite similar to that of Walter Howato.

Carver unknown, pueblo and year unknown. 15" J. Bialac Collection.

the same plate.[18] He is painted in multi-colored stripes with a single horn or topknot on the crown of the head, the characteristic appearance of the Kwirena among the eastern pueblos.

Other terms used are Voth's reference to the Koshari as the Naka because of their cornhusk earrings,[19] while Colton called them the Hano Chuku-wai-upkia.[20] Numerous spelling variations exist for each of these names. Bandelier designated them the Delight Makers.[21]

In doll form, the Koshari may be represented with a blue face, the Sakwa Koshari (fig. 30); a body that is painted entirely yellow, the Sikya Koshari (fig. 31); or decorated with stripes of many colors, the Kuwan Koshari (fig. 32). When the Koshari comes to drum, he may be dressed in whatever fashion is considered suitable for the occasion (fig. 33).

Before the Paiyakyamu lapsed in Stephen's time, it had a permanent chief who belonged to the Cottonwood (Kachina) clan of the Hano Tewa. This group possessed remnants of altar furnishings and considered themselves to be the leaders and the fathers of the kachinas. They recruited by initiating those they had cured of an illness or through trespass of their "ash house," as did the Tewa of the northern Rio Grande. However, by the 1890s, the chief had no fetishes and no other ceremonial paraphernalia was passed on to

his replacement. Consequently, the society disappeared following his death.[22]

Despite the familiarity of the Koshari's general appearance, there are some elements of his dress and actions that are not as well known but that are equally essential to his purpose. The horns are of untanned sheepskin stuffed with a heavy grass and tasseled at the tips with crinkled cornhusk strips referred to as *sohua,* mist.[23] A tuft of these same corn husks hangs at either ear and is undoubtedly the reason for the name "Naka."

The horns are painted with charcoal and kaolin, and any bit of string or cloth is used to hold the headpiece in place. These are kept from year to year and reconditioned whenever they are worn. The man's hair is pulled up behind in the usual hair knot, although it is said that the Tewa used to wrap their hair around a stick and tie it with string to make the horns.[24] Preferably, the body is painted black with corn smut, but soot can also be used. Kaolin provides the white stripes. The black line that encircles the eyes is continued from the outer corners across the temple, while the line around the mouth continues across the jaw to the ear.

Their moccasins are as old and worn as their breechclouts and the blankets they wear rolled up and wrapped about their hips. Each Koshari wears a pouch of prayer meal around his neck, and slung over his right shoulder is a "journey food" bandoleer, the usual piece of yucca string or yarn with a small piece of piki bread and a sprig of piñon fastened to it.[25] Normally they also have two or three animal hooves that serve as a rattle worn at either the ankle or, sometimes, below the knee. Their leader can be identified part of

The Koshari are also known as the Hano Clowns or the Hano Gluttons. This latter name is suggested by their inordinate eating of just about anything. In this instance the Koshari on the left is about to eat a watermelon, probably by himself. The one on the right is attempting to read a book but the pages have only one letter on each, which may account for the puzzled look on his face. (left) David Huma, Tewa,1985. 5" Frank and Patricia Marie Collection. (right) Carver unknown, pueblo and year unknown. 5" Frank and Patricia Marie Collection.

42

the time by the fact that he carries a dried water fowl, usually a coot or mud hen, which he refers to as his "sister," stuffed in the back of the rolled blanket tied about his waist.

Like the Hopi Tsutskutu, the Koshari are seen only during the spring and summer dances and then only in the afternoons. Although they may roister a bit on their way to the plaza from the kiva, their official entrance is always over the roof tops, to represent their coming over the clouds to the Hopi mesas.[26] As do the Tsukuwimkya, they spring up at the edge of the roof above the dancing kachinas and announce their presence with great yells before making their descent with as much noise, awkwardness, and foolishness as they can muster. Upon entering the plaza, they almost immediately discover the small spruce tree that has been planted at one end of the court; rush to embrace it, referring to it as a *sipapuni* (place of emergence); and wildly fling prayer meal on it before hanging their skimpy bandoleers over its branches. Once the bandoleers have been hung on the tree, they address themselves to making their "house," as do the Tsukuwimkya. Anyone who walks through this ash house is initiated as a member of the Koshari group.

Above: Koshari with a Tsuku in their midst in front of the small spruce tree. Courtesy of John Wilson

Koshari and Tsutskutu playing tug of war in the plaza.
Courtesy of John Wilson

At this point, the female relatives of the Koshari bring great quantities of food to the clowns, who place it around the small spruce tree with loud shouts of thanks and appreciation. They begin to eat in the most gluttonous manner they can manage, as Fewkes called them, the Hano Gluttons. After perfunctory attention to their meal, they apply themselves to their real purpose, which is not only to amuse the people but through humor, to emphasize how ridiculous improper behavior can be, whether on the part of the villagers, outsiders, or the priests. Nothing and no one is spared. They are an object lesson of "Life as it should not be lived."[27] The result is always a reinforcement of village mores and tradition hidden under the guise of amusement.

Their departure, usually on the second day, also follows a set procedure that requires a lashing with willow branches by the Warrior Kachinas and a dousing with water, to "bring the rains." This includes a mock confession of imaginary events, often using a close relative as the butt of the tales, that concludes the performance.

Clowning episodes by the Koshari are the same as those engaged in by the Tsutskutu. However, the Koshari seem to engage in more contests. One of their favorites involves tying an equal number of Koshari together by their penises and then proclaiming a tug of war. Or, grasping the foot of the one in front of them, they attempt to hop around the plaza.

At other times, they hold improbable curing rites. In one such episode, two Piptuka come into the plaza dressed as an old Navajo medicine man and his wife. Two of the Koshari announce that they have been having pains in their stomachs and legs. Speaking only

THE TEWA CLOWN, THE KOSHARI
The large figure is a typical Koshari. There are many variations of this clown such as (top to bottom) the Sakwa or Blue Koshari; Sikya, the Yellow Koshari; the Kuwan or Colorful Koshari; and the Koshari Drummer.

Fig. 34.
Kaisale

Navajo, the medicine man says that he can cure them for a fee, which the clowns run to get from a nearby house. The medicine man seats them on a blanket and faces them to the east. Then, seating himself behind the Koshari, he takes out his small rattle and sings a Navajo curing song as he burlesques the ceremony. He ties a string around their heads and upper arms and stuffs juniper twigs into the binding while his "wife" grinds grass on a metate nearby. As he sings, he takes an eagle feather from his medicine bag and strokes their backs and bellies and blows the evil off the end of the feather. Then he takes a short wand and presses it against different parts of the clowns' bodies.

The medicine man puts away the wand and takes out a small board marked with soot and presses this to their backs. Next, he takes a large cloth ball wrapped with string, and, standing behind his patients, throws it against their backs, knocking the wind out of them, which is always vastly amusing to the audience. Finally, he pushes the clowns down full length on their faces, yanks off their breechclouts, and taking a large handful of the grass pulp from the metate, slaps it on their buttocks. He then pretends to insert a large feather into their anus. However, the quill is stuck between the clowns' legs, which leaves the feather upright.

All the other clowns demand to be treated, and the medicine man soon has all of them lying in the plaza with feathers waving

Fig. 35.
Tihu

Fig. 36.
Kachina

in the breeze. He then gathers up his fee and he and his wife leave the plaza.[28]

Current events provide the Koshari with other material. In the mid-sixties, when the efforts of the United States space program were devoted to putting a man on the moon, the clowns in the village of Hotevilla on Third Mesa decided that they would also fire a rocket to the moon. They secured a model rocket and after great consultations and haranguings, set it up in the plaza. Then, with proper fanfare, they placed a mouse in the rocket and fired it. In a plume of smoke, the rocket vanished out over the mesa's edge and the clowns returned to their usual tomfoolery. Sometime later the rocket returned, coming over the house tops to drop into the plaza among the clowns. Shrieking excitedly and exclaiming over its return, they rushed to pick it up. When they finally thought to open it to see how the mouse had fared, they found not only the mouse, but also a big chunk of green cheese! Because the Hopi have a legend of a gourd that was used to fly to the moon, the conversations of the clowns played on the efforts of NASA and the value of the Hopi method couched in a manner that caused gales of laughter throughout the entire episode.

Fig. 37.
Santa Ana

Fig. 38.
San Felipe

Fig. 39.
San Felipe

Fig. 40.
Zia

Fig. 41.
Isleta

Fig. 42.
Santo Domingo

Fig. 43.
San Ildefonso

KAISALE OR KWIRENA

Left: The Winter Clown (Kaisale). The standing figure, playing with the watermelon, wears the single topknot of hair topped with prairie falcon feathers and the multi-colored stripes characteristic of this clown. In addition, he is wearing a cowboy boot on one foot and the other is bare. The kneeling figure of Kaisale is engaged in some tomfoolery as he is holding a cigarette behind his back.

(left) Darin Calnimptewa, pueblo unknown, 1990. 14" S. Simpson Collection. (right) Nate Ahownewa, pueblo and year unknown. 6" J. Bialac Collection.

The Kwirena are the winter aspect of the Kossa just as the Koshari are the summer group. Although present in virtually every pueblo, the Kwirena pale beside the ubiquitous Koshari, Son of the Sun. This may in part be because clowning is not the most important aspect of the Kwirena. In some pueblos, they are concerned with sprouting or germination of corn, whereas the Koshari help with its maturation.[29] It is only in the far west at Hopi where they come as clowns for the kachinas[30] and are known as the Kaisale, a name that is used as an alternate term for the Koshari at neighboring Zuni.[31]

Two of the elements with which the Kwirena (fig. 34) are most often associated are the moon and cold, or winter. In fact, the single horn that adorns the top of the Kwirena's head is frequently referred to as ice, an icicle, or an "ice mother." The presence of this single horn is the outstanding mark of the Kwirena regardless of how the face or body is painted. At the tip of the horn are long shreds of corn husks and always the feathers of the small prairie falcon. With the exception of Isleta, where the Kwirena may be yellow, red, or white,[32] the Hopi are the only ones with polychromatic horizontal painting (fig. 35, *tihu* and fig. 36, kachina).[33] At almost all of the other pueblos, the Kwirena are painted white or gray, often with dark vertical stripes, a pattern that is visually closer to the body painting of the Newekwe at Zuni (figs. 37–43).

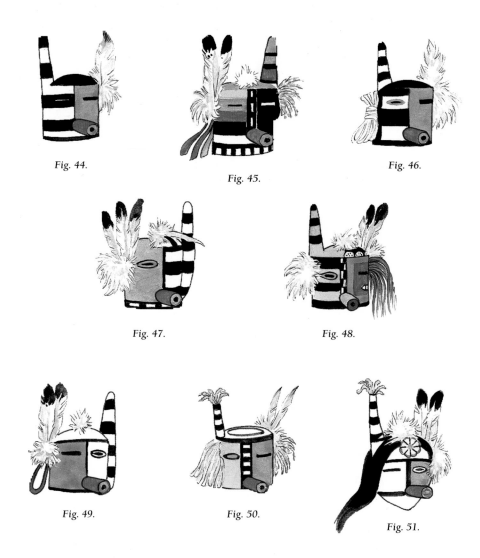

Fig. 44.

Fig. 45.

Fig. 46.

Fig. 47.

Fig. 48.

Fig. 49.

Fig. 50.

Fig. 51.

NATUKVIKA KACHINA

Figs. 44-51.
Natukvika variations

Right: This Kachina is
most often called the Half
Koshari, although his
proper name is Natukvika.
The story has it that he
was hit by lightning and
then put back together, but
the parts didn't match.
Carver unknown, pueblo and year
unknown. 10" E. Lowry Collection.

In recent years, a figure that resembles a Koshari, or rather, part of a Koshari, has appeared in the Hopi plazas. This individual is half-Koshari, half-kachina and is referred to as Natukvika. It is said that the deity Sotuknangu struck him with lightning and then, when he put him back together again, failed to get the right parts together.[34] There are a number of variations of this individual but he is always considered to be a kachina dancer, not a clown (figs. 44–50). Another variation appears as the Bayachum (fig. 51), or drummer, who may come with a variety of plaza dancers. It is possible that each of these impersonations has a specific name or accompanies a particular kachina but there is scant information about them.

Left: The drummer for the Natukvika Kachina is called Bayachum. He is also known as the Corn Boy Drummer. Drummers can come with almost any costume and this one is no exception, as he is wearing what appears to be a Plains Indian vest and leggings.

Duane Lacapa, pueblo unknown, 1991. 12" J. Bialac Collection.

Right: This drum-playing Kaisale shows a variation in the way his face is painted. It is almost always painted in stripes across the eyes and mouth rather than the circular arrangement shown in this clown.

Albert Silas, pueblo and year unknown. 14" J. Bialac Collection.

THE TEWA CLOWN, THE KAISALE
The large figure is a characteristic Kaisale with the feather that identifies him. When he is made as a doll (upper left) he is usually a simplified version of the real Kaisale (lower left). There are numerous variations in the Rio Grande pueblos like (right, top to bottom) Santa Ana, San Felipe (two figures), Zia, Isleta, Santo Domingo, and San Ildefonso.

KOSHARI-LIKE KACHINAS
There is a variety of kachinas called Natukvika that resemble the Koshari. Half of the face is that of a clown and the other half a kachina. These drawings illustrate many variations on this theme. The head on the bottom right is a type that comes as a drummer.

PAIYATAMU, THE SUN YOUTH

Above: The young men of the village at the spring during the Flute Dance at Oraibi.

Courtesy of John Wilson

Left: Different aspects of Paiyatamu as seen in the real world. At bottom are two Koshari; upper left is a Red-Striped Clown; upper right is a Kaisale.

DESPITE THE VARIETY OF SACRED CLOWNS FOUND AMONG THE Hopi, both the Tsutskutu and the Kossa have the same supernatural patron, Paiyatamu, the Sun Youth. Although his name may change slightly in each pueblo, Paiyatamu, the handsome supernatural, is also present from the Northern Tewa of San Juan to Zuni, as well as at the Hopi villages. Variations on his name include Payetemu, Paiyachiamu, Paiyakyamu, Paiyetemo, Patyabo, and Tapaiyachiamu. Only at Hopi is he known both as Paiyatamu and Taiowa. But at each village he is considered to be the patron of the sacred clowns. There are threads of similarity as well that show in the origin stories of Paiyetemu.

Among the Northern Tewa at the upper end of the Rio Grande, one origin story is told concerning the emergence of the people from the sacred lake into this world. Half of them, the Winter People, went hunting through the mountains. The others, the Summer People, went along the river bottoms, growing all manner of green things. But before long, many people in both groups began to die, and their head men at last decided that they must be missing something or someone. The people were told to return to the lake from which they had emerged. When they arrived at the lake, meetings were held and it was discovered that the Kossa had not emerged with the people. To correct this, the Hunt Chief (*Pikqe Sendo*) made a figurine of Tapaiyachiamu (Paiyatamu), the God of the Kossa, from sweet cornmeal dough. When he had done this, the Kossa emerged. The Hunt Chief painted them with white stripes and put corn husk points on their heads and told them to make fun so the people would be happy and get well.[1]

A story from Zuni tells of three old people, two men and a woman, who were members of the first society, the Shiwannakwe or Rain Society. These three sat alone and sad when the Twin War Gods chanced upon them and decided to help the situation. They spoke to the old people and said, "Take rubbings from your skin and make a little ball. Cover it with a blanket and sing over it." This the old people did and when they removed the blanket, they found a little boy who was so full of life that he was never still. He laughed and joked and mimicked everyone and everything around him, even the most sacred rituals. He said and did anything that came to his mind without regard for its effect. In his heedless way he amused the old people, who were thankful for this presence, and they called him Paiyatamu, the Sun Youth, or *Bitsitsi*, the first of the Zuni clown society, the *Newekwe*.[2]

Among the Keresan pueblos, a similar tale tells that Paiyatamu was created by Iyatiku, the Earth Mother, in the same manner as in the Zuni story. However, in this tale he was created not as Paiyatamu but as his alter ego, the Koshari, and was given a rainbow to play upon.[3]

In each of these instances the personage referred to is either the supernatural patron of the clowns, Paiyatamu, or a clown always associated with him. Among the far western pueblos, there are other links that are easily recognized in the larger context of Hopi and Zuni social structures.

At Hopi, control of all village functions is divided among four male societies, the One-Horned, *Kwakwantu*; the *Wuwuchim*; the Two-Horned, *A-ahltu*; and the Singers, *Tataokyamu*, all of which are mutually exclusive.[4] They are ranked by the order of their emergence from the Underworld and every young man must belong to one. Taiowa (Paiyatamu), the patron of the Wuwuchim Society, is also the Son of the Sun and a musician and jester whose original home was in a spring in the white mountain at the northwest end of the Zuni Mountains.[5]

At Zuni, the first society to emerge was the Rain-making Society (*Shiwannakwe*), and second, the Clowns (*Newekwe*).[6] In this second group, one member, the personage called Bitsitsi, is important. In

Right: The Payata-um Kachina is an Oraibi version of a Cochiti society figure that combines elements of both the Koshari and the Paiyatam' clowns, but is not to be considered a clown.

Henry Shelton, Oraibi, 1991. 16"
S. Simpson Collection.

58

myth, the Newekwe traveled near Ash Spring one day when they met a being called Kokothlanna with whom they exchanged cere- monial knowledge on curing. When they parted, this being per- suaded Bitsitsi to come live with him in the spring and become the musician and jester to the Sun. Bitsitsi agreed to this and thereafter was known as Paiyatamu, the Son of the Sun.[7]

The common threads in these myths are the creation of a being for the purpose of amusement whose name is Youth or Sun Youth and who is closely related to the sun. He and those associated with him are believed to be the second group to emerge from the Under- world, or are the second in importance. He is either a patron or an alter ego of the clowns.

Other early Pueblo tales of Paiyatamu that are concerned with his appearance, nature, powers, and association offer different and perhaps clearer perceptions of his nature.

Among the eastern pueblos, the Koshari are believed to occupy a home just south of where the Sun rises, while the Kwirena's house is just to the north, and Paiyatamu's home is thought to lie between these two and close to the Sun. Cochiti is an exception, however, as there Paiyatamu's home is not in the east, but rather, close to the village, reflecting their conception of the center of the world.[8] To the west among the Hopi and Zuni, where water takes on greater importance, the location of Paiyatamu's home is under a spring. There, as with many other kachina-like beings, whether patrons of a clowning or a curing society, they are often found living under water. In this respect Paiyatamu is similar to the kachinas but is not thought of as being one.

In almost every instance, he is believed to be a handsome young man with a healthy libido, a prototype for lovers, one who plays a flute from which comes not only music that causes the flow- ers to bloom but also draws the butterflies of the world to him. At Zuni, according to Stevenson, he is believed to be a diminutive, flower-crowned being who, with his flute (*sho'kona*), can cause the flowers to bloom. His home is in a spring that is constantly covered with a rainbow at the base of Shun'lekaiya, a mesa near Corn Mountain.[9] He is also known there by the even more fitting name of Sun Musician, *Yatokia Paiyatamu*.[10]

Stevenson maintained that at Zuni, the Paiyatamu of the Newekwe, the jester and musician, should not be confused with the Paiyatamu, god of music, flowers, and butterflies who lives in the spring of Shun'le'kaiya and is so conspicuous in the myth of the Corn Maidens.[11] Nevertheless, one of Paiyatamu's most consistent traits in the western pueblos is not only his association with corn,

Corn Maidens, Corn Dances, and corn grinding but also with Flute or Water dances, with dew, springs, and other forms of moisture. His persona consistently reflects both of the attributes that Stevenson separated, making it seem more reasonable that the figure is one with a multi-purpose nature, a nexus of associated concepts relating to corn-growing and water.

In the migration stories that Cushing related for Zuni he seems to feel that they are one and the same, for it is Paiyatamu who claims to be the foster father of the Corn Maidens and who instructs the Zuni people in the proper care of and respect for corn. Furthermore, the story of the creation of the Corn Maidens that Cushing recorded is virtually a description of the Palhik'o ceremony still performed at Hopi by the women's society, the Mamzrau, who are so closely related to the informal clowns, the Wuwuchim, and Taiowa. Cushing also referred to Paiyatamu as the God of Dew and Dawn, the protector of the Corn Maidens, the father of the Newekwe, and one who reputedly introduced the Flute Dance to the Zuni. This water-bringing ceremony, the Flute Dance, was a duplication of the Corn Dance. When it was performed, it was said that mist rose from the branches of willow held by the maidens in the dance, the butterflies of summer appeared, and the dress of the rainbow was seen, all attributes of Paiyatamu.[12]

Despite the fact that Paiyatamu is considered to be the protector of the Corn Maidens, it is he and his society members whose inordinate desire for the Corn Maidens caused them to run away and hide. (It is hard not to see this as a romanticized version of a conflict between the performance of the Corn ceremony and the Flute ceremony.) But then in the role of Bitsitsi, it is Paiyatamu who finds the Corn Maidens and persuades them to return to Zuni, an occurrence dramatized in the Molawia Ceremony.[13] "Paiyatuma . . . was tall and beautiful, and banded with his own mists."[14] Superficially, this sequence makes it appear that there are two personages, yet so much is shared by the two that it is difficult not to believe that they are one and the same with multiple attributes.

One of the characteristics of all Pueblo sacred clowns is the fact that they often speak in reverse or behave in opposites. For example, clowns will tell the men to do the women's work and the women to hunt rabbits, or declare that the most respected elders in the village are guilty of obscene actions. They will announce that anticipated events are not going to happen when they will, making each pronouncement as ridiculous as possible. Saying the opposite of what is meant is often mentioned in the literature and is characteristic of all clowns and their patrons: the Paiyakyamu at Hopi, the Newekwe of Zuni, the Koshari of Santa Ana, the Black Eyes of Isleta, and the Ts'un'tatabo'sh of Jemez to mention a few.[15]

Researchers have advanced many reasons, both psychological and anthropological, for this behavior. It is, however, an attribute shared with many supernaturals and is most probably the result of at least two factors: First, inhabitants of the Underworld are contrary in every respect and would, of course, speak backwards or in a fashion opposite to what the normal person expects. As Cushing relates, "No longer a clown speaking and doing reversals of meanings . . . as do his children (followers) of the Newekwe, today . . . was Paiyatuma."[16] Second, of course, the clowns' purpose is amusing the audience, and reversed actions and speech are inherently funny—the more inappropriate the better.

However, less attention has been paid to the reasonable supposition that form may also be reversed. The supernatural who is the epitome of male beauty and is surrounded by the better things of life may be represented by clowns who wear inappropriate clothing or almost nothing and who are disgustingly rude and crude and are in fact the opposite of their patron. The relationship of Paiyatamu—whose attributes speak of the beautiful things in Pueblo life—with the coarseness of the clowns is one that can only be recognized in terms of the interrelationship of opposites, the concept of dipolarity, that is such a strong element in Pueblo thinking. There is, in fact, another statement in Cushing's *Zuni Creation Myths* that relates just such a dual nature for Paiyatamu.

"Of a sudden, for the sun was rising, they heard Paiyatuma in his daylight mood and *thlimnan* [changed from his Underworld form to his opposite nature, that of the clown]. Thoughtless and loud, uncouth of mouth was he, as he took his way along the outskirts of the village. Joking was he, as today joke fearlessly of the fearful, his children the Newekwe, for all his words and deeds were reversals . . . of themselves and of his sacred being."[17]

It would appear that the Kossa or the Newekwe of the normal world are the reversal of Paiyatamu, who belongs to the Underworld or more appropriately, the Spirit World, and that he is mutable, depending upon where and when he appears. He is seen in his proper guise in the Corn Grinding Party, under a spring playing his flute, while other young men sing songs for the return of warmth and vegetation and life, and the young women grind corn.[18] His other guise is his antithesis, the crude, obscene clown.

As previously mentioned, Paiyatamu's association with water is emphasized among the western pueblos, where his home is under a spring and he lives in a land of mist, fog, and cloud and uses a rainbow to play on and comes wrapped in bands of mist. The Tewa belief that Paiyatamu is a rain-making spirit is in part indicated by the reference to the cornhusk adornments on the ends of the Koshari horns as *sohua* or mist. The same moisture associations exist for the Kwirena in a different but appropriate form. For example, the Winter People of the northern pueblos, like the Kwirena of Nambé and Tesuque, have "Ice Mothers" that represent their moisture-bringing patron in wintertime. So strong is this belief that there is a story told about a woman of the eastern pueblos who had been one of the Kossa and sold her images of Paiyatamu to a storekeeper. The man kept them and treated them with respect. When he died, rain fell and rainbows spanned the spring and on the fourth day it rained again.[19]

Yellow clowns, yellow clays, yellow flowers, yellow pollen, yellow hands and feet: yellow, the sun's color, is the one most often associated with Paiyatamu. Yellow pigment is used by both the Hopi Wuwuchim and Tataokyamu societies, whose patron is Taiowa, particularly when they appear as informal clowns. Taiowa's altar is hung with yellow flowers, especially sunflowers. Taiowa, as patron of all the Hopi clowns and the Wuwuchim and Tataokyamu societies, is also by extension a patron of the women's Mamzrau society, for the Mamzrau and Wuwuchim are considered to be brother-and-sister organizations. In addition, Taiowa and Mamzrau are sometimes referred to as a brother and sister and the Sun as their father.[20] At Hopi, when the Mamzrau women dance as the Water-Drinking Maidens, they paint their feet and hands yellow; the men's societies powder their faces with corn meal to make themselves beautiful like their patron, Taiowa.[21]

Paiyatamu's medicine, best known at Zuni, is supposed to come from the hearts of butterflies, dragonflies, and the flowers of the *te'nats'ali*, a plant with blossoms of the colors that represent the six directions, or the petals of any yellow flower. Yellow pollen is used when praying to the Sun Youth.[22] At Zuni, yellow ochre from Kachina Lake is ground and mixed with the dried petals of yellow flowers by the curing societies to make Paiyatamu flower meal.[23] Just before Zuni kachina dancers leave the kiva, they are sprayed with Paiyatamu meal by the kiva chief in order to make the dancers beautiful and attractive.

As a musician Paiyatamu most frequently carries and plays the flute, particularly the long one with a bell-shaped end. When the Flute Ceremony is held among the Hopi, a contingent of handsome men arrayed in their most beautiful costumes, wearing a large sun

symbol on their backs, goes to the springs.[24] The flutes are played
only at the spring and is most surely a dramatization of the
Paiyatamu legend in the Corn Grinding performance of Hopi and
Zuni. Paiyatamu is also associated with drums. Large drums in
Cochiti[25] and Santo Domingo are even called "Paiyatamu." These
are not the ordinary small drums but the very large ones that are
used in dances. At both Hopi and Zuni, these large wooden drums
are thought to contain either butterflies or strong men's voices and
if used improperly can make the women go "crazy."[26]

At Zia, when a youth is initiated into the Hunt Society, he
receives an image of Paiyatamu along with other fetishes.[28] At Jemez,
offerings to Paiyatamu are kept in a shrine that contains the heads
of mountain lions and bears as well as miniature hunting tools. In
a similar fashion, at Zuni, the skulls of prey animals are kept in the
same cave shrine with offerings to Paiyatamu, the Sun Youth.[29]
Likewise on the Hopi Second Mesa, deer and mountain sheep
skulls and bones are kept with offerings to Paiyatamu.

While these fragments do not completely delineate Paiyatamu
or Taiowa, they do present a generalized perception of the elements
of importance embodied in or associated with this personage who
represents the ultimate of happiness, namely: the color yellow in
any form, representing life or the Sun and his light; the procreation
of humans; youth; the sounds and sights of summer, such as butterflies and flowers, flute and drum music; moisture as springs and
mists, ice and frost, but not necessarily of rain; and the growth of
corn and animals.

Paiyatamu is also linked to hunting. It is said that he has control of animals and insects and he was created by the Hunt Chief
among the Northern Tewa.[27] This may account for his inclusion in
hunting rites and shrines, for he is a patron of both the Koshari and
the Kwirena. It may be a function of his appearance as a Kwirena,
the winter clown, who travels with the people who hunt in the
mountains.

THE PAIYATA-UM KACHINA
This kachina, which is not a clown, bears resemblance to both the Paiyatam' and Koshari clowns.

THE KOYEMSI

Above: Koyemsi throwing
presents to the crowd.

Courtesy of John Wilson

Left: The Powamu Koyemsi could be called a Talavai-i Koyemsi just as easily, for he comes at dawn. This Koyemsi appears on the last day of Powamu, running through the village and delivering bean sprouts and presents to the young, uninitiated children.

Henry Shelton, Oraibi, 1986. 12"
S. Simpson Collection.

PROBABLY THE BEST-KNOWN FIGURE IN THE PUEBLO PANTHEON is the Koyemsi, or as he is better known, the Mudhead. Simply dressed in a black kilt made from a woman's old dress that covers his clay-reddened body, with a black kerchief around his neck and a mud-colored head with knobs on it, the Koyemsi presents a comical appearance. Despite the fact that he is easily recognizable and his names are well known, neither Koyemsi nor Mudhead is his proper name. Both are nicknames, the former from Zuni and the latter from English. Among the Hopi, his proper name is Tachukti or Tatsi'oktu; at Zuni, it is Molanhaktu.[1] Each term means "Ball-on-Head."[2] At Tewa, he is referred to as Huntamehlepo.[3]

The Zuni nickname of Koyemshi, or "husband,"[4] arose from their function as husbandrymen (in the archaic sense of one who cares for a flock) to the kachinas. This name accompanied these personages when they passed into several of the eastern pueblos. There, they became the G'o'maiowish at Acoma, Go'maiyawish at Zia, and Go'maiyawash at Santa Ana. At Laguna he is known as Gumeyoish, and Gumeyoishi at Jemez. None of the other eastern pueblos appear to have a masked representation of the Koyemshi.[5]

*A Piptuka walking
around a group of
Koyemsi at Oraibi,
circa 1903.*

Courtesy of John Wilson

To the west, among the Hopi, both the name and persona were
adopted as the *Koyemsi*, probably during the interval from 1860 to
1880, when it gradually supplanted the indigenous Tachukti or
Ball-on-Head. Today, only the Zuni-style Koyemsi appears to be
present among the Hopi, with the possible exception of the Toson
Koyemsi.

Early traders and collectors, unaware of a proper name,
referred to this figure as "Mud Head" or "Muddy Head" because of
the color of the mask and what appeared to be balls of mud stuck
on the head in various places. Because the appearance was comical
it was assumed to be a clown. However, just as its real name is neither Koyemsi nor Mudhead, neither is its purpose the buffoon-like
being the term clown implies. Rather, the Koyemsi serves a multi-
plicity of purposes. Even though he is amusing and can perform
hilarious antics or play ingenious games—both with the audience
and other Koyemsi—he is far more than a clown. He can be a
curer, a magician, a dance director, a warrior, a messenger, a sage,
or a fool. He may come stripped down as a member of the
Pashiwawash, the Racing Kachinas or Runners, to challenge the
young men of the village.[6] He may also come in the guise of a hun-
dred different kachinas that are in no way considered to be clowns.[7]

Much of Koyemsi behavior, both at Zuni and in the Hopi villages that have borrowed the personage, is explained in the origin
legend. At Zuni, where the only origin myth of any strength is to be
found, there are always just ten Koyemshi, a father and his children. Mythically born of an incestuous union between brother and
sister, the nine children resemble their father, who in the agony

Above: These four Koyemsi represent just a few of the functions in which a Koyemsi might be engaged. The one on the left is carrying a small Koyemsi doll in his arms. The next is carrying piggyback a smaller Koyemsi, a Koyemsi'kima. The third, a Pushun' Koyemsi, is drumming, while the last one is sitting making a doll.

(left) Leonard Shupla, Sr., Shungopovi, 1986. 10" S. Simpson Collection. (2nd left) Elvin Namoki, Walpi, 1985. 10" E. Lowry Collection. (3rd) Sheldon Talas, Tewa, 1987. 11" S. Simpson Collection. (right) Marlin Huma, Sr., pueblo unknown, 1987. 10" S. Simpson Collection.

of remorse at his misdeed, rolled about and beat his head on the ground, raising great welts and covering himself with dirt to create the tragic image of the Mudhead. In appearance, his children are men, yet they are witless and sexless as well. Because of the stigma of their birth, they are forever barred by the deities from belonging to either the world of men or that of the kachinas and must always remain assistants and yeomen to the kachinas and messengers to men and live apart. As Cushing's interpretation states, "Silly were they, yet wise as the gods and high priests. Like simpletons or the crazed they spoke nonsense one instant and wise words and prophecies the next and as such they became the attendants and interpreters of the kachinas."[8]

At Hopi, just as at Zuni, the Koyemsi are not considered to be kachinas and they live in a separate location at Wenima, one that is especially their own, near the kachinas' home but not of it.[9] So too do the Zuni believe that the Koyemshi live near the kachinas' home at Kothluwala but are not a part of them.[10]

Their difference from humans and kachinas at Zuni is most apparent, for not only are they masked but their actions and even their very names are inverted. Thus one whose name is The Speaker merely babbles or says nothing, the reverse of what is

desired for the office of a Speaker. And so it is with each and every one. They are of the opposite nature to that indicated by their names and they speak the reverse of what they mean, as do all from the Underworld. Despite such simple behavior, the Koyemshi are very dangerous·and it is the height of foolhardiness to deny them anything, or even to speak of doing so. Not only do they speak to the Ancient Ones, they speak for them, and in the knobs on their heads they carry all the seeds needed and used by the Zuni as well as dust from the tracks of the inhabitants of the pueblo.[11]

In the Koyemsis' most common role as interlocutors between kachinas and humans, they announce impending events, translate requests, give directions, and present other information, albeit in a garbled or inverted fashion such as telling the men to do women's work and vice versa. As foils for the kachinas, they may intensify emotion, as when, at Zuni, they shriek that they see blood when children are whipped during their initiation into the Kachina Cult. They may also use humor to lighten an overly serious moment or merely to amuse an audience during a boring interlude.[12] However, despite strong religious restrictions and the many serious tasks that they are required to perform at Zuni, their usual behavior is that of witless simpletons.

Among the Hopi, the Koyemsi have no fixed organization with chiefs, members, and altar paraphernalia as they do at Zuni.[13] Instead they are informally selected from kiva memberships on the basis of ceremonial need. Parsons was of the opinion that in earlier times, a Koyemsi organization might have antedated the introduction of the Koyemsi mask, and that possibly the organization represented a war scout group. There are, however, few indications among the Hopi Koyemsi to support this contention.

There are numerous differences between the actions of the clowns and those of the Koyemsi. When the sacred clowns enter the mesa villages, they come in over the rooftops, "from the clouds," say the Hopi, and announce their presence with loud yells. The Hopi Koyemsi may enter the plaza in the same manner as the kachinas, at ground level. An exception is when the Koyemsi announce the beginning of the *Anktioni,* or Repeat Dances, after Powamu; they appear on the rooftops ringing cowbells and gesticulating wildly.[14] The Koyemsi always arrive masked, while the sacred clowns never come in that guise. While the Koshari and the Tsukuwimkya both make an ash "house" by drawing an outline in ashes on the ground and initiating anyone who blunders across it, the Koyemsi neither build such a "house" nor initiate by trespass.[15]

Left: Three different examples of the Sweet-Cornmeal-Tasting Mudheads, or Toson Koyemsi, the ones who sample the meal the little girls have ground for the Soyoko. The Toson Koyemsi in the middle is very much like the early Tachukti, or indigenous Ball-On-Head.

(left) Jonathan Day, Hotevilla, 1983. 11" S. Simpson Collection. (middle) Herbert Talaheftewa, Shungopovi, 1960-1970. 9" E. Lowry Collection. (right) Randall Sahmie, pueblo unknown, 1987. 8" S. Simpson Collection.

A line of Koyemsi entering a village prior to a dance.

Courtesy of John Wilson

The Koyemsi may appear with the kachinas as a chorus or as a single drummer but no Tsuku ever functions seriously as a drummer, nor do they come as a chorus. Occasionally a Koshari may drum for the kachinas. Further, the Koyemsi may enter the plaza as a dance group of their own but while clowns may seem to come as such a group, it is a transient resemblance, a sham performance.

The Koyemsi also appear in performances where they do feats of magic, wrestle with the Water Serpents, engage in games with ritualized content, appear as puppets, accompany the Sio Shalako,[16] and fetch wood.[17] Clowns perform none of these activities. In addition, a clown performance invariably ends with a purificatory whipping by kachinas, but this never occurs with the Koyemsi who, when they retire, may be given *pahos* (prayersticks) by the clowns[18] and be sprinkled with cornmeal by the kiva chiefs.[19] Although both the Koyemsi and the clowns talk while the kachinas do not, it is only the Koyemsi who pause and deliver a serious harangue in the midst of their tomfoolery, for they are spokesmen for spiritual rules and values.

When the Koyemsi play, their actions are somewhat different from those of the sacred clowns. The play most often consists of guessing games of one sort or another with members of the audience. Stephen describes one episode in the kiva where four cones were placed one on top of the other and a woman was selected from the audience to try to lift the stack to a height and carry it around the room without dropping one. The reward was a large pile of valuable items. When no one succeeded in doing this, the stack was reduced to two items and the reward to bundles of corn.

The Kuikuinaka is an unusual Koyemsi and a very important one. Although his visible role is starting the line of kachinas dancing with a shake of his rattle, he is considered to be a representative of Muyingwa, the God of Germination. When he is made as a doll he usually has a staff in his right hand that is carried only by important figures. He does not carry this when he comes in the line of kachinas. The slight differences between the dolls of Henry Shelton and his uncle, Kyrate Tuvahoema, are interesting as they indicate changes that take place through time. (left) Henry Shelton, Oraibi, 1990. 17" S. Simpson Collection. (middle) Kyrate Tuvehoema, Moencopi, 1930–1940. 13" E. Comins Collection. (right) Maker unknown. Cloth doll, Shungopovi, 1960-1970. 15" E. Lowry Collection.

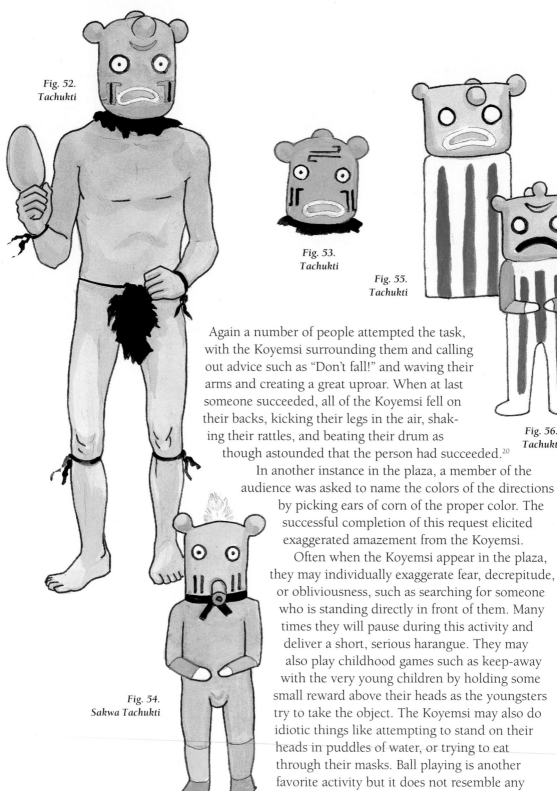

Fig. 52.
Tachukti

Fig. 53.
Tachukti

Fig. 55.
Tachukti

Fig. 56.
Tachukti

Fig. 54.
Sakwa Tachukti

Again a number of people attempted the task, with the Koyemsi surrounding them and calling out advice such as "Don't fall!" and waving their arms and creating a great uproar. When at last someone succeeded, all of the Koyemsi fell on their backs, kicking their legs in the air, shaking their rattles, and beating their drum as though astounded that the person had succeeded.[20]

In another instance in the plaza, a member of the audience was asked to name the colors of the directions by picking ears of corn of the proper color. The successful completion of this request elicited exaggerated amazement from the Koyemsi.

Often when the Koyemsi appear in the plaza, they may individually exaggerate fear, decrepitude, or obliviousness, such as searching for someone who is standing directly in front of them. Many times they will pause during this activity and deliver a short, serious harangue. They may also play childhood games such as keep-away with the very young children by holding some small reward above their heads as the youngsters try to take the object. The Koyemsi may also do idiotic things like attempting to stand on their heads in puddles of water, or trying to eat through their masks. Ball playing is another favorite activity but it does not resemble any

organized game. Rather, it consists of trying to hit one another with some sort of ball. When hit, the Koyemsi invariably exhibits exaggerated pain. Frequently the smaller Koyemsi will harass some of the most fearful kachinas, such as Chaveyo, or lead others like Owangazrozro around on a rope, skipping out of reach when the kachinas turn upon their tormentors.

THE TACHUKTI

Indigenous Hopi Koyemsi

Before the turn of the century, the Hopi had two varieties of the Ball-on-Head beings. One was either a native version, or at least one acquired in the far distant past, called Tachukti (figs. 52–56). The other was a more recent addition that copied one or more of the ten Zuni Koyemshi (figs. 57–66). The Reverend H. R. Voth, in his notes from the 1890s at Oraibi, spoke of the native figure as Tatcioqtu and noted the presence of two separate forms and that one was supplanting the other.[21] On First Mesa, Alexander M. Stephen at about the same time called the indigenous being Tachukti in his journals.[22] Both of these names mean the same, differing only in spelling. Stephen also remarked on the presence of the Hopi and Zuni forms and the difficulty of separating them. The second figure, borrowed from the Zuni, was called the Sio (Zuni)

Above: Soyoko and Toson Koyemsi at kiva hatch with their collected loot.

Courtesy of University of New Mexico Photo Archives

Fig. 57.
Awan Pekwin

Fig. 58.
Awan Pithlashiwanni

Fig. 59.
Muyapona

Fig. 60.
Ecotshi

Koyemsi by the Hopi; by the last decade of the 1800s, it had almost completely supplanted the indigenous version.

The reasons for the change from the indigenous Hopi form to that of Zuni may have been due in part to the prim Victorian mores of government employees, missionaries, and educators who found the almost non-existent costume of the Tachukti offensive and sought to enforce government policies banning such figures. It may just as easily have been that the Zuni Koyemshi afforded a relaxation of restrictive behavior accompanying the local version by shifting to a related personage. A third possibility, and probably the most likely, was a combination of the loss of ceremonialists in the mid-nineteenth century due to the devastating smallpox epidemics of 1853, 1857, and 1859; raids by the Apache, Navajo, and misguided elements of the United States Army; accompanied by a severe drought. The amount of disruption caused by the loss of population and established life ways as the remaining Hopi fled for survival to neighboring areas is incalculable. Regardless of what accounted for the demise of the Tachukti, little is known of his attributes other than his existence as witnessed by a few early ethnographers and the presence of a few *tihu* in the older museum collections.

These early observers—who recognized that there were the two forms and named them accordingly—had great difficulty keeping them separated. Voth had the following to say concerning them: "Different varieties of the Koyemsi Kachina[sic] exist among the Hopi. One was introduced from the Zunis and is known by the Zuni name, Koyemsi. The typical features of this variety are the nodules

*Figs. 57-65, above:
These portray the
Zuni Koyemshi.*

Fig. 61.
Nalashi

Fig. 62.
Itsepasha

Fig. 63.
Kalutsi

Fig. 64.
Posuki

Fig. 65.
Tsalashi

and long appendages on top of the mask, to which are fastened turkey feathers, *nakwakwosis,* and furthermore, a small snout on the mask. They also wear kilts. The typical features of the original Hopi kachina [sic] of this kind are the following: three balls or nodules on top of the mask, from which it takes its name, Tatcioqto (Ball Head); marks of sprouting beans on the cheeks and forehead of the mask, a ring of cloth representing the lips instead of a snout, and instead of a kilt, a piece of cloth in front of the body only. Furthermore the body is painted with a light brown clay instead of a reddish clay, as is the case with the Zuni at present. However, the typical features of either of these are almost invariably mixed not only in kachinas [sic], but also in the *tihus* representing them. *Tihus* showing the typical features of either of these two varieties only, are extremely rare. Both varieties, or rather a mixture of the two, may be seen on many occasions on the plaza as well as in kiva dances. They are mostly as jesters, some of their acts being very coarse and obscene."[23]

In addition to Voth, both Stephen and Owens remark on the same fact of recognizing differences but being unable to separate the two.[24]

The Tachukti (fig. 52) were characterized by a tan color made from a local clay, rather than the pinkish tone of clay from the Sacred Lake used by the Zuni Koyemshi. Their garb consisted of a rag around the neck and a bit of cloth suspended in front so that it was an apron rather than a breechclout, leaving the buttocks completely bare. It was the mask itself, however, that demonstrated the greatest differences. The eyes were white ringed with black and on the forehead and cheeks were symbols referred to as "bean sprouts."[25]

In the earliest *tihu*, the symbols are more often the parallel marks attributed to Pöökanghoya, the Little War God,[26] or the angled mark that represents the prairie falcon's wing.[27] Both of these elements lend some credence to Parson's contention that this group of clowns had a warrior function elsewhere at one time.[28]

The mouth was usually a ring of cloth that could be elongated into an oval shape with downturned corners, or simply a cloth flap. The head, which was usually more rectangular than the Zuni-inspired Koyemsi, was decorated with only three nodules, one at either side above where the ears would normally be and the other at the rear of the head. Occasionally, a fourth ball was added on the forehead.

Of great interest among the older *tihu* is the presence of three Tachukti with blue-painted heads (fig. 53). The earliest of these dolls was collected by Stevenson between 1880 and 1884 and has no forehead markings.[29] Voth has the following to say about the two blue-headed dolls that he collected between 1893 and 1898: "The distinguishing features of this Koyemsi as a Hopi Koyemsi or Tatcioqto are the blue mask with the three double bean sprout marks, and the peculiar arrangement of the breechclout which leaves the buttocks bare. For the latter reason this Koyemsi appears very seldom now, but almost always the Koyemsi adopted from the Zunis, the loins of which are fully covered. The kachina [sic] carries a *tiponi* in the left hand." [30]

The presence of a *tiponi*, an empowering device,[31] in the hands of a Tachukti would seem to indicate that this particular personage was a principal chief, head of a fraternity, or held some position of importance. Such individuals place their *tiponi* upon altars during ceremonies. However, he also resembles the contemporary Mong, or Chief Koyemsi, who is portrayed holding a *tiponi* but is not important. Unfortunately, there is insufficient information to do more than speculate about the role or the status of the blue-headed Tachukti.

The other Tachukti have tan heads and bodies and are virtually indistinguishable from the Sio (Zuni) Koyemshi except that the eyes are usually white encircled with black, or entirely white rather than tan. A few of these older *tihu* have forearms and calves painted alternately yellow and blue (fig. 54) or the body coated white with vertical red stripes (figs. 55–56) in the manner of the flat dolls presented to infants. Occasionally one

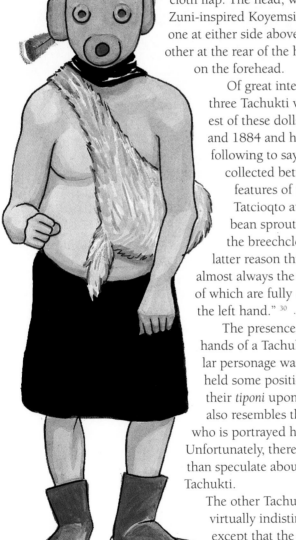

Fig. 66.
Zuni Awan Tatshu

will have the crown of the head painted entirely blue. The heads of those with the "bean sprout" marks on the face are almost identical with the present-day Toson or Sweet-Cornmeal-Tasting Koyemsi (figs. 67–68). The costume of the contemporary Toson Koyemsi, however, is very elaborate in contrast to this earlier figure.

The Zuni Koyemshi adopted by the Hopi did not retain its original character for long. It was rather quickly changed in several ways to more fully reflect local needs. The restrictions limiting the Koyemshi to ten in number was discarded so this personage could then appear as a single drummer, a chorus of thirty, or in even greater numbers as a separate dance group. It is possible that there was a requirement of unlimited numbers for the Tachukti before it was supplanted by the Koyemsi.

The varied functions performed by the Zuni Koyemshi as a group were also separated and individualized, with appropriate changes in costume and mask. The features of the Hopi Koyemsi (fig. 69) changed, as did the shape and arrangement of the balls on the head. The small, limp horns on the crown of the head of the Zuni Koyemshi (fig. 66) became a single thick, rigid, vertical spike, while the knobs on the sides might appear with pendulous lobes, all with turkey feathers dangling from them. Gaping mouths became snouts or other shapes. The eyes might be painted on or made from extended tubes sliced off at an angle or simple buttons with slits. Some of these individualized Koyemsi acquired distinctive names, others were grouped by function, while still others remained unnamed. The end result was that many varieties of Koyemsi developed at Hopi.

THE KOYEMSI

There are a number of Koyemsi who differ in appearance and come for specific purposes and do not behave in a clownish manner. These are the Kuikuinaka, the Powamu or Talavai-i Koyemsi, the Kipok Koyemsi, Powak Koyemsi, as well as the changeable Tuvé Koyemsi who may come to dance with a variety of kachinas. There are others who have equally important purposes but whose actions are nearly always accompanied by clowning. Because the functions of the Koyemsi span so many variations, it is not possible to separate them into clowning or non-clowning groups. Instead their activities must be considered as a continuum made obvious by appearance but ranging in function from serious to comic.

Kuikuinaka Koyemsi

The Kuikuinaka Koyemsi (fig. 70) is not a clown.[32] He differs from other Koyemsi in that he is dressed in an embroidered robe and a white shirt with a black bandoleer. He carries a long staff or cane in his left hand and a rattle in his right. On the back of his head he wears a knot of parrot feathers with a vertical bundle of long red macaw tail feathers extending above it. His name, Kuikuinaka, means "He starts it," referring to the fact that he starts the kachinas' songs and is the song leader when he comes with the kachinas and dances in line with them.[33] He is usually positioned in the middle of the dance line. Although his role appears simple, he represents Muyingwa, the Hopi deity of germination.[34]

Toson Koyemsi

The Toson, or Sweet-Cornmeal-Tasting Koyemsi, considered to be the uncle of the Nataskas, comes with the Ogres, the Sosoyoktu, around Powamu time on First and Second Mesas. One of the Toson Koyemsi may accompany the Ogre Woman, Soyok' Mana, on Second Mesa when she goes around the village. To the little girls, Soyok' Mana hands out bits of corn to be ground, and gives strips of yucca to the little boys, to be used to trap "deer" (actually mice) for the Ogres when they return (fig. 67).

Eight days later, the Sosoyoktu return in force, demanding the food the children have prepared for them. When a tiny mouse on the end of a stick is timidly held out a partially open door, the Ogres howl their outrage, demanding more food and threatening to take the child instead. The Soyok' Mana says that because the

Fig. 67.
Toson

Fig. 68.
Toson

Fig. 69.
Koyemsi

Fig. 70.
Kuikuinaka

*Fig. 71.
Powamu*

youngsters have not behaved properly no one wants them and they would enjoy eating them. The family protests and excuses are offered for the children with promises that they will do better in the future. More food is presented until the Ogres are satisfied. When the little girls put out the sweet cornmeal they have ground, the Toson Koyemsi (fig. 68) taste it, and then argue and bargain in a burlesque manner, seeming to consult with the Sosoyoktu until at last they decide whether or not to accept the proffered gifts. Frequently during these interchanges, the children are forced to re-enact their misdeeds of the past year before the Ogres will pass on to the next house. While this activity is going on, the Toson Koyemsi and their cohorts, the Sikya Heheya, busily haul the offerings back to one of the kivas.[35]

Late in the evening, the men of the village arrange an impromptu dance and lure the Ogres and the accompanying Toson Koyemsi and Heheya into joining them. The erotic behavior of the Heheya toward the "women" (played by the younger boys) and the complete inability of the Ogre Woman to dance properly are convulsively funny to the audience. As the twilight deepens, the men of the village suddenly fall upon the party of Ogres and strip them of all their booty, taking even their clothes, before driving them over the mesa edge and out of the village. The entire episode is an object lesson for the children. It defines their roles, and stresses that they must do their work and perform it properly as well as behave in a reliable manner. If they do, even though threatened, both family and village will come to their assistance. Thus, through wise and peaceable means, they can persevere in life.[36]

Above right: Koyemsi getting a woman from the audience to guess what is under the canvas.

Courtesy of John Wilson

It is quite possible that the Toson Koyemsi is the modern version of the Tachukti. The primary difference between the two is in their costume. In contrast to the almost complete nudity of the early Tachukti, the contemporary Second Mesa Toson Koyemsi is garbed in a woman's dress and belt, with a kilt (*pitkuna*) worn as a breechclout. Black stockings, garters, and ordinary moccasins are worn on the legs and feet with a colored kerchief around the neck. During their first appearance they are wrapped in blankets. However, the faces of both are almost identical: the "bean sprout" symbol is painted on their cheeks, and a quarter moon, placed horizontally, on their foreheads. The only other Koyemsi that wears these cheek symbols is the Kipok Koyemsi and here, more often than not, they are the straight tracks of Puukonghoya rather than the "hooked" bean sprout. In addition, the Kipok Koyemsi never wears the forehead symbol. The annular eyes and mouth of both the Tachukti and the Toson Koyemsi are the only ones that are white or light-colored. However, the Tachukti's are usually black-rimmed. On Third Mesa, this type of Koyemsi is replaced by the Heheya.[37]

Powamu, the Talavai-i Koyemsi

The Powamu (fig. 71), a Talavai-i Koyemsi who may appear at dawn on the ninth or final day of the Powamu ceremony, does not function as a clown. When he comes, he joins the many kachinas that busy themselves carrying bean sprouts to each household in the village. During the Powamu ceremony, which takes place in mid-winter, usually February, buckets and tubs are brought into the kivas and filled with sand. Beans are planted in these and the kivas heated to force-grow the beans in the winter chill. On the final day, long before dawn, the bean sprouts are harvested and each man sets aside a small handful. The remainder are taken to his house, where the women hide them. Returning to the kiva, he takes the small bundle and ties it to the presents that he has prepared for his children or favorite relatives. Girls and women are given kachina dolls, while the little boys receive bows and arrows, rattles, and other similar things. In each kiva, several members dress and assume the identity of a kachina they prefer to deliver the presents.[38] Quite often, one of these impersonations will be the Powamu Koyemsi.

Running through the village, the many kachinas deliver the presents and the bean sprouts to the different homes. Upon receiving their presents, the children are told that the small bunch of sprouts will grow and feed the entire family if put into a pot and

cooked, because they come from the kachinas. When the sprouts are set to cook, the others that have been hidden away are secretly added, to make a very large pot of bean-sprout stew.

During this part of the ceremony, the Powamu Koyemsi is dressed not as an ordinary Koyemsi but as a kachina, with blue armlets, a red bandoleer, dance kilt with sash, and a woman's belt. A foxskin dangles behind him and garters with sleigh bells are fastened below each knee so that the Koyemsi can be heard coming and going through the village.

Kipok Koyemsi

Fig. 72.
Kipok

Fig. 73.
Kipok

The Kipok Koyemsi (figs. 72–73) are fighters, not clowns, and they do not speak. When the Tsutskut or the Koshari are clowning in the plazas, their actions become more and more outrageous until at last the Warrior Kachinas appear.[39] Each of these warriors may be a different impersonation such as the Great Horned Owl Kachina, the Kipok Koyemsi, the Crow, or any of a dozen others.[40] First, a single fighting kachina appears in one of the passages into the plaza from which he watches for a while and then disappears. A short time later, more fighters arrive and the original kachina will enter the plaza and appear to talk to the leader of the clowns before leaving once more. As the clowns heedlessly continue their antics, the Warrior Kachinas return in force to punish the

Right: The Kipok Koyemsi comes as a warrior to punish the misbehavior of the clowns with the yucca whips he carries in each hand.

Carver unknown, pueblo and year unknown. 14" J. Jacka Collection.

clowns for their transgressions. These fighting kachinas tumble the clowns into a pile and whip them with willow branches, then douse them with water in a purification rite.

The Kipok, War Cry, or War Leader Koyemsi[41] was originally called the Powak (Wizard or Witch) Koyemsi before it was named Kipok. Believed to be a true *powaka* or witch personage, it is said to have first been seen in a dream by Bert Fredericks of Old Oraibi. In this dream he went to *Powalunga*, the meeting place of witches, and was pursued by these figures until he returned home by awakening from the dream. He then made the first image of the Kipok Koyemsi.[42] His brother, Charles Fredericks, also saw this Koyemsi in a dream when the witches attempted to draw him to his death. He too made a Kipok Koyemsi and kept it in either his house or the home of another Hopi. However, before either of these men dreamed of this kachina, it had appeared in 1893 on First Mesa.[43] Today, the Kipok Koyemsi is not thought of as a witch.

Presumably, the Kipok Koyemsi is an ordinary Mudhead until he takes on the role of fighter against the clowns. Then he alters his appearance by adding a fan of feathers at the rear of his head and painting a black-and-white band, a war path, across his eyes. However, the earliest known *tihu* of the Kipok Koyemsi is dressed as a Snake Dancer with a black torso, crossed bandoleers, and both a Snake belt and kilt. In addition, he wears the warrior track marks on his face.[44] The same figure on Second Mesa (fig. 72) comes dressed in a white shirt and black pants with a sash and blue armlets.[45] Yet another from First Mesa comes with his bare body painted like a Koyemsi but wearing high boots, blue armlets, and a breechclout (fig. 73).

Powak Koyemsi

The Powak Koyemsi (fig. 74) is not to be confused with the Kipok Koyemsi, who was initially called by the same name when he first appeared. This Koyemsi is known as either a magician or a witch. He usually appears as the head of a group of Mudheads and manages their actions. He comes barefoot and holding a basket that contains seeds. He is also capable of magical tricks such as making a feather dance in a bowl.[46]

Tuvé Koyemsi

One of the most confusing aspects of the Koyemsi is his ability to substitute for kachinas. The ones who do this are called either Tuvé

Left: The Tuvé Koyemsi is one who can take the place of a kachina due to some happenstance that has prevented the proper impersonation from being presented. In this instance the kachina being replaced is a Sakwa' Hoté.

Carver unknown, pueblo and year unknown. 17" E. Lowry Collection.

Fig. 74.
Powak Koyemsi

Fig. 75.
Toson Koyemsi (var.)

Fig. 76.
Hu Koyemsi

Fig. 77.
Honan Koyemsi

(decorated) or Kuwan (colorful) Koyemsi.[47] They are costumed as a particular kachina but wear a Koyemsi mask. They can represent a wide variety of kachinas, possibly all of them, and behave just as those with whom they appear.

It is not uncommon for an individual who has been unable to practice or who was late in preparing in some fashion to don a Koyemsi mask in order to take part in a dance.[48]

In other instances, the Koyemsi actually takes the place of a missing individual and performs his ritual. An example of this kind of substitution occurred in 1893 on First Mesa. In an unusual occurrence, five children were initiated into the Kachina Cult in the plaza at Tewa by a substitute or Tuvé who was attired as a Kipok Koyemsi (fig. 76). The circumstances were that although the kachina mother, Tumash, and her two sons, the Tungwub Kachinas, had appeared the night before, it was decided that they could not come the next

Fig. 78.
Puukong Koyemsi

Fig. 79.
Ka-e Koyemsi

Fig. 80.
Angak' Koyemsi

Fig. 81.
Wakas Koyemsi

day because there were no Walpi children to be initiated. The whipper, a Tuvé Koyemsi,[49] represented the Hu or Tungwub Kachina. In a similar occurrence on Second Mesa in 1985, Ahöl' Mana failed to appear during the Soyal ceremony and her place was taken by a Tuvé Koyemsi, in this instance a Koyemsi Mana (fig. 90).[50]

In most cases, the role is not that important and the Koyemsi replaces the kachina simply by donning his garb and placing identifying symbols on his head. Examples of this are the cheek marks of a Badger Kachina (fig. 77), the crossed feathers of a Corn Dancer (fig. 79) or the face markings and horns of the Cow Kachina (fig. 81). He may come as one of the Two Little War Gods (fig. 78) or the favored Long-Hair Kachina (fig. 80). Finally, in some instances, the Tuvé Koyemsi may come with the face markings of one of the other varieties of Koyemsi and the body paint of a kachina (fig. 75).

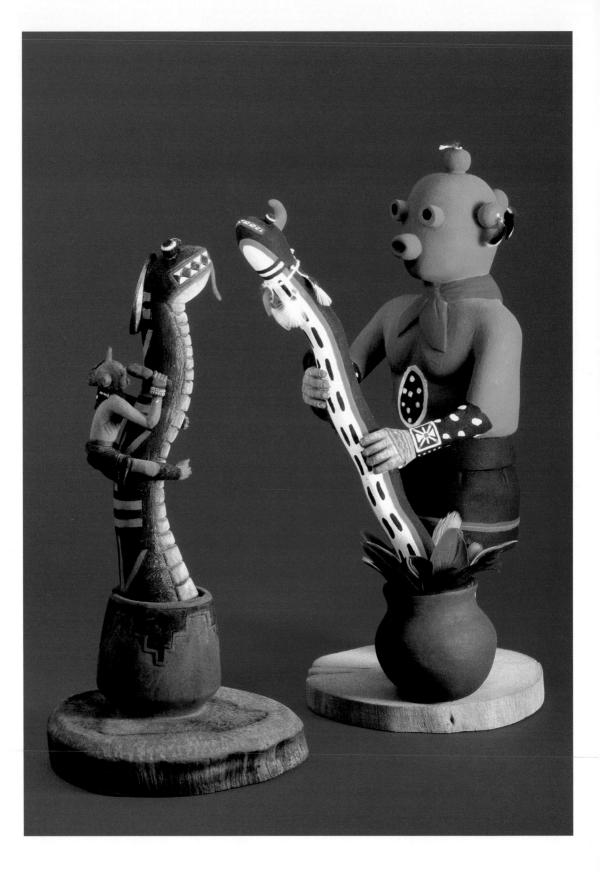

Mongwi Koyemsi

The Mongwi Koyemsi (fig. 82), whose behavior is often clown-like, usually appears as an elderly personage with a white mustache and, more often than not, a large central horn on the crown of his head. Although he wears the standard Koyemsi garb, he often drapes a white buckskin over his shoulders. If he also wears a Navajo or Chimayo blanket about his hips, he can then be called a Kwivi Koyemsi regardless of the other aspects of his appearance.[51] A black circle filled with white dots is painted on the chest of the Mongwi Koyemsi and some Hopi say this represents his heart, while others contend that it is his rattle.[52] Among the eastern pueblos this is a society mark. However, it is a mark found on Ogres, Angry, and Animal kachinas as well.

When the Mongwi Koyemsi appears he frequently carries what seems to be either a *tiponi* or a large bundle of feathers, and he often acts as though he were a chief. He considers himself to be very important and in charge of the other Koyemsi and from this attitude come his nicknames, "Big Boss" or "Bragger."[53]

Fig. 82.
Mong Koyemsi

Fig. 83.
Koyemsi with
Palölökong

Koyemsi with Palölökong

In the kiva during the Water Serpent ceremony, the Koyemsi may accompany a magic performance wherein the serpent appears to rise from a large jar. As it emerges, the Koyemsi grapple with it and even appear to ride on its back (fig. 83).[54] In this instance, the Koyemsi do not usually behave in a clownish manner nor do they appear to be a specific type.

Left: The Koyemsi are closely associated with Palölökong, the Feathered Water Serpent. In one of the performances, Palölökong is presented as a stick puppet who rises out of a jar. The Koyemsi appear to wrestle with him as he emerges from the jar but are knocked to the ground. A smaller Koyemsi may even get on his back and try to ride him before he too is thrown off.

(left) Jim Fred, Bakavi, year unknown. 10" J. Bialac Collection.
(right) Clifford Lomaheftewa, Shungopovi, 1987. 12"
S. Simpson Collection.

Fig. 84.
Pushun' Koyemsi

Fig. 85.
Koyemsi'kima

Pushun' Koyemsi

One of the Koyemsi's most frequent roles is that of drummer for
the kachina dancers (fig. 84). While he attends to business during
the actual dance he may engage in a bit of mild horseplay with the
clowns between sets of the dance.

Koyemsi'kima

The Koyemsi frequently ride piggyback upon one another (fig. 85).
This behavior, although unexplained at present, is distinctive of
the Koyemsi.

Tatcimu, Hishot, and Gumeyoish Koyemsi

There are other types of Koyemsi who make occasional appear-
ances but about whom little is known. The Tatatsimu or Hopok
Koyemsi (fig. 86) usually come as one of a pair and play with a
ball on a string. He dresses in a breechclout and a white shirtlike
garment.[55] The Hishot or Hisat Koyemsi (fig. 87) differs from most

Fig. 86.
Tatsimu

Fig. 87.
Hishot

Fig. 88.
Gumeyoish

others in that he has white pothook eyes and a curved white line
on either cheek as well as a red kachina-style snout. He also wears
high boots.[56]

Another, the Gumeyoish (fig. 88), is usually referred to as a
curing Koyemsi and may represent an eastern pueblo figure or one
from Laguna. He comes with a bull-roarer[57] in his right hand and
a small hoop and pole, devices for foretelling the future, in his left.
Strands of blue and white yarn hang from his ears, three white bars
are painted on each cheek, and he wears a rather elaborate collar.[58]

Fig. 89.
Koyemsihoya

Koyemsihoya

A recent innovation, the Koyemsihoya (fig. 89) is a ceremonial puppet who dances to a drum beat and gestures when properly manipulated. The person controlling the puppet always impersonates a Koyemsi himself during the ceremony. The puppet is believed to be a small, mischievous boy, a light-hearted trouble-maker, who often plays with the children. Although he plays pranks on the Hopi he is not considered to be a clown but rather, an important spirit to whom prayers are offered.[59]

Koyemsi Mana

Occasionally the Koyemsi are accompanied by a female version (fig. 90), always impersonated by a man, who may on occasion appear as one of the more important or Chief kachinas.[60]

Fig. 90.
Koyemsi Mana

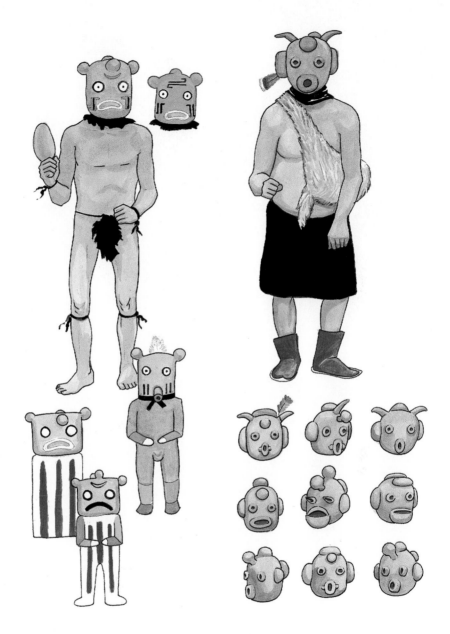

THE HOPI TACHUKTI AND THE ZUNI KOYEMSHI
The earliest known Hopi Koyemsi were called Tachukti (upper left) and occasionally came with a blue head. The early dolls (lower left) are distinctively different from the Zuni Koyemshi, resembling the Hopi Toson Koyemsi more closely. There are ten Zuni Koyemshi, including the father Awan Tatshu (upper right), as well as (lower right) the Speaker Awan Pekwin, the Bow Priest Awan Pithlashiwanni, the Wearer of Eyelets of Invisibility Muyapona, the Bat Eshotsi, the Aged One Nalashi, the Glum Kalutsi, the Infant Suwitsana, the Pouter Posuki, and the Old Youth Tsathlashi.

VARIETIES OF HOPI KOYEMSI
The typical Hopi Koyemsi is the large figure. Surrounding him (top row, left to right) are the Kuikuinaka Koyemsi, the Powamu Koyemsi, two versions of the Kipok Koyemsi, the Mong Koyemsi, and the Koyemsi Mana. In the bottom row, left to right, are two varieties of the Toson Koyemsi, an old-style or ancient Hishot Koyemsi, a Laguna Gumeyoish, and a Hopi Ball Player or Tatcimu Koyemsi.

OTHER VARIETIES OF HOPI KOYEMSI

Many of the Koyemsi vary through their actions as the Pushun' Koyemsi or Drumming Koyemsi and the Koyemsi'kima or Piggyback Koyemsi (upper left). The Wizard or Powak Koyemsi (center row, far left), the Puppet or Koyemsihoya (center), and the Koyemsi with Palölökong (upper right) are all kiva performances. The line of figures, listed left to right, are the Tuvé Koyemsi, who may represent kachinas such as this version of Toson Koyemsi, who came as a dancer; this Kipok Koyemsi, who came as a Hu Kachina; a Badger Koyemsi; one who came as a Puukong Koyemsi; a Ka-e or Corn Dancer Koyemsi; a Long-Haired Kachina dancer; and a Wakas or Cow Kachina.

6

THE PIPTUYAKYAMU

Above: A Piptuka and Piptu' Wuhti in the plaza at Oraibi.
Courtesy of Bethel College

Left: The Tasavu is a caricature of a Navajo. He is one of the buffoonish Piptuka who is portrayed so often that he has become a stable characterization. His actions are those of a Piptuka yet the constancy of his appearance resembles that of the true clowns.
Wilfred Tewawina, Moencopi, year unknown. 17" J. Bialac Collection.

THE PIPTUYAKYAMU ARE AN ASSEMBLAGE OF MEN WHO TEMPOrarily band together to present an impromptu performance or skit. Their name is derived from *pitu,* a word that means "to come [or] arrived," thus, Piptuka roughly means "one who keeps coming." In addition, they are known as Napoa'dei by the Tewa, Talasuna at Mishongnovi, and Pifteka on the remainder of Second Mesa.[1] The ethnologist Stephen, in discussing them, seldom used the word Piptuka or Piptuyakyamu, preferring instead to call them "Grotesques."[2] Parsons continued this nomenclature, saying it was used "consistently to distinguish them from the other burlesquing groups that are referred to as clowns."[3]

Grotesque is a word most commonly used in art to describe figures or designs characterized by distortion or exaggeration. Thus the word can be loosely applied to a caricature of a person. However, "buffoon" is a more appropriate term for the Piptuyakyamu, as the meaning is very precise. A buffoon is "a person who amuses with low or coarse jests, vulgar and antic posturing, or any other form of indecent humor" (OED), and that is definitely the nature of the humor presented by the Piptuka.

Two Tsutskutu with a Piptuka in the plaza at Oraibi during a Navajo dance.

The Piptuka are not sacred clowns,[4] as are the Kossa and the Tsukuwimkya, nor are they the equivalent to the Koyemsi, despite the amusement they afford. They do not follow a prescribed routine when they come nor do they have a traditional appearance, other than a tendency to whiten their bodies and faces. The fact that the Piptuyakyamu may occasionally come masked has often led to the conclusion that they are kachinas, as masks are such an integral part of the kachina costume. However, a mask is not the only positive identification of a kachina. The Hopi Powamu dancer is a kachina whether he wears a mask or not. The Palhik' Mana, on the other hand, is not considered to be a kachina and yet, on Third Mesa, she appears masked. Neither are the masked Koyemsi to be considered kachinas.

The face and costume of the Piptuyakyamu are infinitely variable because they depend on the skit being presented (figs. 91–97). If the demand is for a tourist, the Piptuka will be attired in a costume that caricatures the visitor. If it is a Navajo or Paiute, a mask may be used and the costume changed to pick out the quintessence of the individual or group being satirized.

In almost every instance, the humor of the buffoons is based upon some incident that has happened in the village or to some village member. This is usually presented in the most obscene manner possible and if it does not lend itself to such treatment, the Piptuka will invent some way of converting it to the form of humor most appreciated. The use of the clowns as "straight men" or foils for the humor of the Piptuyakyamu is a consistent trait. Where the action of the sacred clowns always follows a traditional pattern, that of the

The figure on the left is a Piptuka who is representing a Navajo although he does not have the usual striped body and face. The kneeling figures are of a White Cloud Clown on the left who is shooting dice with a Tsuku. On the right is a Piptuka of a farmer with his canteen of water and his hoe ready for work in the fields.

(left) Larson Onsae, Shungopovi, year unknown. 15" E. Comins Collection. (double figure) Ronald Honyouti, Bakavi, 1987. 7" S. Simpson Collection. (right) Wilson Vina, pueblo unknown, 1992. 10" S. Simpson Collection.

Left: Piptu' Wuhti mounting a hobbled burro with the help of Tsutskutu in the plaza at Sichomovi, circa 1919.

Courtesy of Anna Kopta and University of New Mexico Photo Archives

Above: A Piptuka and two clowns in the plaza at Oraibi during the 1890s.

Courtesy of Bethel College

Piptuyakyamu never does. Although the content of their "play" is much the same, the humor of the Piptuka is usually coarser, more current, and of short duration. The skits may require interaction with the clowns or be presented as things apart.

Several years ago, in an outstanding episode, the Piptuyakyamu portrayed the marital difficulties of a young Hopi man who had married a Navajo girl. He brought his new wife home but their marriage was rocky, and their problems echoed through the village at night. When the Piptuyakyamu appeared during the next kachina dance, they proceeded to enact all of the problems of the young couple in full view of the rest of the villagers. The hilarity that accompanied this episode indicated how close to the mark the Piptuyakyamu were in their skit. Almost certainly the couple's actions and arguments were on a far quieter plane thereafter.

Stephen mentioned various episodes with the Piptuka. One such skit from First Mesa described by him involved a Piptuka and all of the clowns in a characteristic performance. A Piptuka dressed as an American school teacher arrived (fig. 91). He carried a cane and a book and sported very black whiskers on his whitened face. He lined up the clowns as school boys and had them sing. Setting them to work on lessons, he pulled off the clowns' breechclouts.

*Tsutskutu involved
in some play in the
Oraibi plaza. A Piptuka
wanders around in
the background.*

Courtesy of Bethel College

The "schoolmaster" then had them bend over and touch their toes and while they were doing this he inserted a twig crosswise between their buttocks. When they stood up they cried out and feigned great pain. But when the schoolmaster started to leave the plaza the clowns caught him and yanked down his pants to expose a large bladder penis. They then made him bend over and inserted a twig as he had done to them and made him walk around the plaza with his pants down around his ankles.[5] During the late nineteenth and early twentieth centuries, the Hopi had many problems with school teachers and their methods of teaching, and this ridicule was obviously directed at them.

Another performance lampooned a typical visitor of the period. Carrying a covered lunch basket, the visitor arrived and effusively shook hands with the Piptuka "girls," giving them lots of scribbled money for their dolls. But when the Piptuka men approached, he ran them off. Out of his basket he took balls of brightly colored cornmeal dough representing candy, and threw it to the clowns for them to fight over.[6] It was a common practice among early visitors to the Hopi to take hard candy when they came and fling it into the group so they would scramble after it. The other activity speaks for itself and was a common theme for both clowns and Piptuyakyamu.

Caricaturing the visitors or workers from the outside world was a favorite skit. In an episode where yet another "American" visited, he came striding along, peering into all of the doors and windows and finally deciding to be a storekeeper (fig. 92). When the other Piptuka came with sheepskins, he would take some and reject others. Some of the clowns he kicked out of his "store" and others

Fig. 91.
Schoolteacher

Fig. 92.
Storekeeper

Fig. 93.
Apache

he knocked about, before making overtures to a Piptuk' Wuhti and taking "her" inside his house. When she came out, she had an armload of calico prints and her enraged "husband" beat her for infidelity until the storekeeper came out with a whip and ran them all away.[7]

Recently, the Piptuyakyamu came dressed as Plains Indians with whitened faces. They carried a large flat drum, and setting it down, they surrounded it, pulled out drumsticks, and began a Plains-style song. (A similar form is the Apache in fig. 93.) The clowns who gathered around in naive curiosity were told by the newcomers that they knew how to control the wind (which had been blowing furiously for weeks!), and for a price would tell the clowns. While the "Plains Indians" were singing, the clowns rushed furiously around, blocking all the doors and windows leading into the plaza. Hardly had they finished before one of the entrances burst open and in rushed the Wind, who raced about the plaza overturning chairs and flinging paper and umbrellas about. The clowns rushed to catch him and then decided that if they fed him

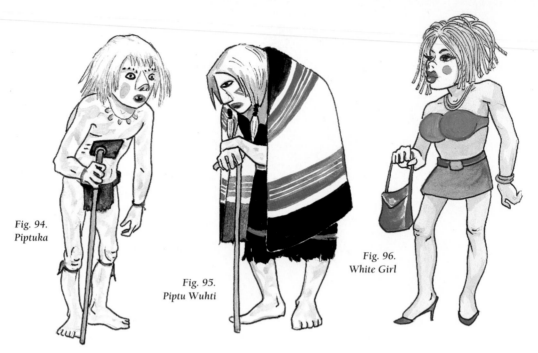

Fig. 94.
Piptuka

Fig. 95.
Piptu Wuhti

Fig. 96.
White Girl

maybe he would go away. They gave him piki bread, watermelon, and other goodies, but as he left he continued to overturn chairs and fling things about. The disgruntled clowns rushed over to berate the buffoons but they had quietly picked up their drum and left with their fee.

When Samuel Barrett was photographing the Hopi villages in 1911, one of the Piptuka entered the plaza at Kiakochomovi impersonating a tourist with a camera and a penchant for learning Hopi. The camera was a five-gallon oil can set on a forked stick. From the can a round object was suspended on a string to represent the bulb of the camera. A piece of old oil cloth was used for a black cloth. In addition the Piptuka carried a large portfolio made of cardboard in which he wrote all of the Hopi words that he heard. After "photographing" for some time he then wandered about the plaza, reading his "notes" aloud and mispronouncing all of the Hopi words he had presumably written, or giving them double meanings, to the immense amusement of the crowd.[8]

Although the Barrett crew were photographing and transcribing data on Hopi actions and words, they apparently did not realize that it was they who were being caricatured by the actions of a Piptuka.

At times the caricatures of the buffoons become so involved that it is difficult to follow the action, as when the Piptuyakyamu put on a burlesque of the women's Mamzrau society burlesquing the men's Wuwuchim society.[9]

Fig. 97.
Kōcha Omau-u Tsuku

Fig. 98.
Tasavu

QUASI CLOWNS

There are a few personages who appear to be neither Tsutskutu nor Piptuyakyamu (figs. 97 and 98). They appear unmasked, as do the true clowns, and reappear fairly often, which is not a characteristic of the Piptuka. The White Cloud Clown and presumably the Yellow Cloud Clown belonged in this category, as do the Yoche and Tasavu, among others. No data exists for the Yellow Cloud Clown (Si-chaiz Tsuku) other than his name. Even the exact appearance of this clown is unknown although it was reputed to be the same as the White Cloud Clown. It seems probable that it is a quasi-clown that has been lost to time. However both the Tasavu or Navajo Clown (fig. 98) and the White Cloud Clown (fig. 97) appear with the Piptuka and both paint their faces white as is the custom of the Piptuyakyamu, but instead of being ephemeral presentations, they always reappear in the same guise. In this respect they are more similar to the clowns than they are to the Piptuyakyamu. They have been called Quasi Clowns as a device to distinguish their differences from both the Tsutskutu and the Piptuyakyamu.

A Piptuka dressed as a Mamzrau dancer in the plaza at Oraibi in the 1890s.

Courtesy of John Wilson

PIPTUKA
Top row: A sampling of the variations in Piptuka are the Tasavu or Navajo, the Kōcha Omau-u or White Cloud Clown, a storekeeper, and a schoolteacher. Bottom row: Most often seen are the old man, and examples of other Indians, in this case, an Apache. Women are often impersonated and range from the white girl to the old Hopi woman.

NOTES

Chapter One: An Overview

1. Titiev: 1972: 255: "Men, like Ned [Don Talayesva] and chief [Wilson Tewaquaptewa], who make frantic efforts to justify everything in their religion, take a defensive attitude. They explain this kind of clowning by reciting a formula. Such doings, they say, 'are worth something. They (the buffoons) are doing it for rain, and for our crops, and for long life.' On the other hand, Tom and most of the younger men who are less concerned with defending their faith admit that such antics are designed merely to amuse the spectators." Different levels of knowledge are represented by these two groups and this is often repeated in other circumstances. The younger generation sees the superficial as the explanation, whereas growth in ceremonial knowledge, acquired through age, will usually produce the formulaic response. It is not a defensive attitude nor an attempt to justify, it is a statement of belief.

2. Thompson: 1950: 130: This was the first time this explanation appeared in print. It has been echoed in recent years by literate Hopi but not by the older generation. However, one of the most vocal adherents is a member of the Eagle Clan, the Third Mesa clan that claims ownership of the clown society.

3. Parsons: 1939: 131: ". . . clowning is a release from ordinary, conventional conduct. It entertains, but it is also dangerous or rather the clowning society is dangerous and fear-inspiring. The clowns are licensed to do what they choose; they are punitive and have express police or warrior functions, particularly getting out dancers or racers or workers on town enterprises like repairing a bridge or getting in a harvest; they are warlike scouts, if not fighters."

4. Stephen: 1936: 182: "Kwuma'lechi, the Kachina clan mother, has the tiponi of the Chuku'wimkya in the house of her daughter Nakwai'yumka, or *had it once*." [emphasis added] This definitely sounds like the tiponi is no longer in use.

   "The Ta'chukti are quite a distinct assemblage from the Chuku'wimkya, the latter have *wi'mi* (ritual objects), the former not. All the Singers and Wu'wuchimtu are Chuku'wimkya, and Ha'ni, Singers' Chief, is chief at Walpi. Ta'hyum (Djasjini) is chief of the Tewa Pai'akyamu, and he confirms what many others have told me, viz. that the Walpi Chuku'wimkya have neither *wi'mi* nor altar, but he has. . ." [January, 1893].

   In July of the same year, Stephen (370-371) reiterates the information about the Tsukuwimkya but presents different information about the Tewa. "The Chuku'wimkya have no chief, altar, or *wi'mi* now. The Zuni have. The last Chuku chief died before Cha'sra [an old man in 1892] can remember. The Pai'akyamu of Tewa have a chief, named Ti'shihoya [Ta'dhyum had relinquished the clown chieftaincy to his younger brother Ti'shihoya between January and April of 1893 and died in August of the same year] but no *wi'mi* (fetiches)." Apparently, the *wi'mi* mentioned in January were not transferred to the younger brother in April and hence this aspect of the Paiyakyamu ceased in 1893. *See also*, following reference.

5. Ibid:182-183: "[B]ut he [Ta'huym] *has*, viz. the little painted cotton blanket (*kwa'chkyabhoya*) which is his altar (*poñ'yaata*), one water jar (*kü'yi si'bvu* i.e. *na'kuyi*, medicine-water jar), and one crook prayer stick." This is the *wi'mi* the Paiyakyamu had in January 1893 that were not passed on to Ti'shihoya.

6. Titiev: 1944: 243, n.6: "The Paiyatamu, a clown society owned by the Eagle clan, formerly met at Hano Kiva [Old Oraibi]. It has not been active for many years."

7. Stephen: 1936: 157: This is a recapitulation of Stephen's information by Parsons in

her Introduction. "There are on First Mesa four clown types: the Ta'chukti, *borrowed from the Koye'mshi of Zuni* [emphasis added], and in the Horned water serpent dance and the Sha'lako dance actually referred to as 'Koyi'msi,' the Pai'yakyamu of the Tewa, the Chükü'wimkya and Pi'ptüyakyamû." Too often, Parsons perceives borrowing as a one-way process and attributes many elements to Zuni because of her familiarity with that pueblo. In this instance, she is correct when stating that the Hopi call the Ta'chukti, the Koyi'msi, when referring to these two dances, as both dances were borrowed from Zuni. She is not correct when she says that all Ta'chukti were borrowed from Zuni as Stephen implies a difference and Voth recognized both a Hopi and Zuni version. He (H. R. Voth: American Museum of Natural History: 1900: #71) states, "While this mask is typically a Zuni, this kachina has long been introduced among the Hopi, where in fact it has rapidly taken the place of the similar Tatcioqtu [Tachukti]."

8. Voth: 1906: CARN. #3165/148. *See also* Tachukti.

9. Mindeleff: 1891: 35-37. *See also* Kossa.

10. Stephen: 1936: 332: "Pi'ptüyakyamû are not Chüküwimkya. Their name is derived from *pi'tü*, to come; anyone takes part, distinctly impromptu performers."

11. Fewkes: 1892: 47-48: Scattered through Fewkes' earlier writing appears to be reference to both Tachukti and Chukuwimkia as Paiyakyamu. Then he says of the Chukuwimkia (page 10): "(Tcukuwympkiyas: At least three kinds of priests may be referred to this assemblage.)" "Tacúkti: which corresponds to the Koyemshi of the Zuni." (page 11): The *Pai-a-kya-mûh* are Tewan *Tcú-ku-wymp-ki-yas.* "They do not wear masks, but instead a closely fitting white cap, with long, straight horn on each side of the head. Corn husks are tied to the apex of these horns, and at the juncture with the cap. . . .The Tewan *Tcú-ku-wymp-ki-yas* more closely resemble the clowns figured by Bourke in the Santo Domingo tablet dance than do the true *Tcú-ku-wymp-ki-yas.*"

"The true *Tcú-ku-wymp-ki-yas* I have seen in Ci-paú-lo-vi. These priests do not wear masks, neither have they the corn husk horns which characterize the *Pai-a-kya-mûh.* Their faces and bodies are painted yellow, and they wear a wig of sheepskin. Across the face, on a level with the eyes, is drawn a red mark, and a second parallel band is painted on the cheeks and lips."

(page 47): "[J]udging from a tí-hu . . .I have . . .: the Hopi *Pai-a-kya-mûh* have the body painted yellow brown, and the black bands are missing. The head is destitute of horns. There are red bands across the face."

12. Ibid:332, 1242, 1272: In name each of these groups, with the exception of the Koyemsi, carries a common suffix, the term *kyamu*. This word is used by both the Hopi and the Tewa for members of a society. The word is believed to be Keresan, the language of the Underworld.

13. Informant: "If the figure is single it is called Tsuku but if there is more than one they are referred to as Chuchkutu." For the sake of clarity in this paper the term Tsutskutu is used rather than Chuchkutu. *Also* Stephen: 1936: 364: "came up from the Horn Kiva a young man (Ka'kapti's brother) arrayed as a Hopi Chuku'wimkya or *sikya* (yellow) Chukuwimkya (both terms are used)"; *also*: 370: "Sikya' Chuku'wimkya or Hopi Chuku'wimkya, the one with wig and with yellow on body."

14. Stephen: 1936: 158: It is Parsons in her Introduction who states that: "All Singers and Wûwûchimtû are *ex officio* Chüküwimkya, and the Singers chief acted as their chief."

15. Stephen: 1936: 370: "Na'somta Chuku'wimkya, those men with the mud body-smear and hair cue [sic] tied up on either side."

16. Informant. *Also*, Stephen: 364-366. *Also* Hieb: 1972: 130.

17. Stephen: 1936: 332, 1272: Stephen believed that the term Paiyakyamu was derived from the Tewa word *pau'ki* or headdress converted to *paiya*. However, Parsons offers a more believable derivation when she relates it to Paiyatemu, the Keresan word for youth. Parsons [Stephen: 1936: 158] gives the following information concerning this group of clowns: "The Pai'yakyamû, which term is almost certainly derived from *payetemu*

Keresan for Youth,* are banded black and white and wear a cornhusk poke headdress. They are the Koshare or Kossa of the East, and at Hano are still called Kossa or Koyala."

However Fewkes (1892:47) offers a confusing note: "The Hopi *Pai-a-kya-mûh* have the body painted yellow brown, and the black bands are wanting. The head is destitute of horns. There are red bands across the face." He does not give a derivation for the term although he adds to the confusion of who the Paiyakyamu are, for between these three authorities the name Paiyakyamu is given to the Koshari/Koyala, the Kwirena/Kaisale, both of whom are called the Kossa, and the Red-Striped Hopi Clown, Paiyatamu, as well as the Tachukti. (ibid: n.*): "At Acoma the K'ashale clowns are also referred to as Pai'yatyamo."

18. Stephen: 157: In her Introduction, Parsons states: "[On First Mesa] The Ta'chûkti, like the Koye'mshi, wear a knobbed mask and carry a fawn skin bag. The black cloth of the women is worn as kilt or breech clout or dress; mask and body are painted with pinkish clay. They sing Zuñi songs, pretend to talk Zuñi, and even make Zuñi prayer-sticks." On pages 169-170, and 174, Stephen describes the Ta'chukti. However, on page 177, he states: "They are members of the Chuku'wimkya, of course, but are always spoken of as Ta'chukti, the ball players."* Stephen is in error, for they are not Chuku'wimkya and no where else does he refer to them as such. Neither does the statement that Ta'chukti refers to ball players rather than balls on the head.

19. Informant: "The White Cloud Clown would be called Kôcha Omau-u." *Also* Colton: 1949: 75.

20. Informant: "The Yellow Cloud Clown can be called either Si-Chuchkutu or Si-chaiz Chuchkutu."

Chapter Two: The Tsukuwimkya

1. Stephen: 1936: 370.

2. Ibid: 553: "[T]he four Pai'akyamu clowns in their typical horn headdress with black and white striped bodies, came out from Pen'dete [kiva], shouting as is their wont and climbing housetops to represent walking over clouds." But Fewkes (1892: 44-45) gives the following information: "They dressed in the first kib-va of Ha'no and emerged from the kib-va entrance with a shout, asking, as if strangers, what was going on in the south. Then they marched to where the dancers were gathered, and, uniting with them, smoked and ate with the Ka-tci-nas. After a short time the dancers put on their masks and made their way to the dancing place east of the rock [at Walpi].* They were closely followed by the *Pai-ak-ya-muh*."

3. Informant.

4. Stephen: 1936: 1213: The Glossary refers to the Chukuwimkya as the Squatting Society and distinct from Tachukti and Paiyakyamu.

5. Ibid: 158.

6. Informant. The clown is called Paiyatamu when the red stripe (*sutangaroki*) or Supai mark is present.

7. Stephen: 1936: 981.

8. Bunzel: 1932: pl. 55b, 1080-1081: The face painting, costume, and hair dress of the Nepaiyatamu are very similar to that of the Wuwuchim members when they come as society members except that it is a masked personage and is considered to be the Ne'wekwe of the kachinas. While it does not pay to carry superficial similarities to great lengths, some interesting comparisons can be noted. The headdress of the Tataokyamu and Wuwuchimtu is a single horn of hair on top of the head when they behave as informal clowns. The same arrangement is present in the headdress of the Nepaiyatamu, who are the informal clowns of the Ne'wekwe. Bunzel says that (page 1082): "[A]t Cochiti the equivalent of the Zuni Ne'wekwe is the Quirana. The Quirana headdress is always a single horn on the top of the head while that of the Koshari is two horns."

9. Owens: 1904: AMNH. #350.9448 and Voth: 1901: pl. LXXIII c. "Paiyatam." *Also* Laboratory of Anthropology, #1357/12.

10. Voth: 1893-1898: FMNH. #65731: "When it comes it dances only in the kiva." *Also* Ibid: AMNH. #50.9488: "Sometimes dances in the plaza in regular dances."

11. Lange: 1968: 479, 497.

12. Stephen: 1936: 449: "Chuku'wimkia with hair *na'sompi* came in over the house tops . . . at Sichomovi." The Soyohim come in and when quite close the clowns spring to their feet ". . . promptly each of them took from a tree a long string or old frayed lariat, at the end of which was fastened the stuffed skin of a prairie dog, and this stuffed skin they cast toward the group of kachina who showed great fear." Parsons (1926: 216) notes that this performance was extinct by 1920, and quotes Crow Wing as saying this event took place during the Pohaha ceremony, and it was the Kossa who threw prairie dogs and squirrels at the kachina, scaring them and making them withdraw. The interchange was kept up all day until the kachina finally went back to their spring homes in the mountains where they were supposed to tell their grandparent. *Also* Parsons: 1939: 395: This is how the Kossa scared them with prairie dogs. Their grandfathers and uncles would become angry and threaten to send flooding rainwater to drown off the prairie dogs.

13. Parsons: 1917: pt. II: 230-231: "These *koko* come from and return to *lutkyanakwe* (*luluwa,* ashes; *tkana,* spring), the spring six or seven miles away from Zuni on the way to Ojo Caliente. It is from here the grey clay is brought for the *newekwe* make-up."

14. Hieb: 1972: 130. "O-ot" is used by Hieb to refer to clowns. This is a term used especially by Third Mesa Hopi.

Chapter Three: The Paiyakyamu or Kossa

1. Mindeleff: 1891: 35-37: "According to Polaka, the son of the principal chief, and himself an enterprising trader who has made many journeys to distant localities . . . and to others, the Hano once lived in seven villages on the Rio Grande, and the village in which his forefathers lived was Tceewage. This it is said, is the same as the present Mexican village of Peña Blanca."

2. Stephen: 1936: 412: "'Long ago, before we had sheep, when we lived in the Northeast at Tewa yonder, we used no skins of any kind as a headdress. We set a stick on each side of the head upright, and round them we lashed our long hair with cotton string wound round and round it. We (Koya'la) are the fathers of all kachina.'"

3. Parsons: 1929: 148: The Kossa were instructed: "'The way you have to do is make fun, so the people will be happy.'"

4. Parsons: 1939: 894.

5. White: 1932a: 17.

6. Parsons: 1939: 439.

7. Lange: 1968: 298: "The Ku-sha'li Society is one of the more widely known Pueblo Indian societies. At Cochiti it is especially famous due to Bandelier's book *The Delight Makers.* . . . Of major concern to the Ku-sha'li Society are weather control, fertility of the animal and plant worlds, and, related to these, the supervision of many ceremonies."

8. Goldfrank: 1927: 34-54.

9. White: 1932b: 97-101: "This society is the equivalent of the Rio Grande Koshare. It is a secret organization with clown and war functions."

10. Parsons: 1939: 170: "When the clowns paint at Zuni . . . they identify themselves with their patron or prototype, Paiyatemu, the Youth, the first of the Ne'wekwe or Koshare, son of Sun Father or of underground Mother." *Also* ibid: 1917: 230: "The first *newekwe* was called *bitsitsi,* * a name not representative today, however, except when he comes out in the *molawia* ceremonial. [P]ayatemu is another name, according to

Stevenson, for *bitsitsi,* and she gives a legend of his relation to the Sun.* *[B]itsitsi* is referred to, I learned, as *yatokia payatemu* (sun musician)."

11. Stephen: 1936: 153, n. 1: Ka'shaili is Zuñi for Koshare, the Keresan clown. Tai'owa is to be identified with Payetemu, the flute-playing Sun youth, patron spirit of the Koshare and of their Zuñi homologues, the Newekwe.

12. Stephen: 1936: 332, 1272.

13. Stephen: 1936: XLIV, n. 2: Parsons states that "In 1920 . . . [t]he chieftaincy of the Kossa clown society (Pai'yakyamu) had lapsed, but it was formerly in the Cottonwood (Kachina) clan" (Parsons: 1925a: 68, n. 112); "the society was recruited through sickness."

14. Stephen: 1936: 158.

15. Ibid: 332.

16. Ibid: 411.

17. Fewkes: 1892: 11: "They are best named gluttons, and their function is the same as the Ta-tcúk-ti." *Also* Fewkes: 1903: plate XXXII.

18. Fewkes: 1903: 178, plate LVIII.

19. Voth: 1896: FMNH/Archives.

20. Colton: 1949: 35.

21. Bandelier: 1890. *Also* Stevenson: 1902: 409: n. a.

22. Parsons: 1925a: 68, n. 112: The obsolescent ceremony of the Koyala (formerly called Kossa) belonged to the Cottonwood clan. Then only members of the ceremony or society played clown. Today men are variously appointed or chosen. *Also* Parsons: 1926: 214-215; Stephen: 1936: 158.

23. Parsons: 1929: 126.

24. Stephen: 1936: 412.

25. Ibid: 489.

26. Ibid: 553: "[T]he four Pai'akyamu clownscame out from Pen'dete [kiva], shouting as is their wont and climbing housetops to represent walking over clouds."

27. Hieb: 1972: 39.

28. Stephen: 1936: 383-384.

29. Parsons: 1925b: 64, n. 1.

30. Informant.

31. Parsons: 1939: 131, n. +.

32. Goldfrank: 1962: 238. *Also* Parsons: 1974: 333.

33. Fewkes: 1903: 126, pls. XXXII, LVIII. *Also* Wright: 1973: 243.

34. Informant.

Chapter Four: Paiyatamu, the Sun Youth

1. Parsons: 1929: 148-149.

2. Ibid: 1917: 229-230.

3. Ibid: 1920: 114, and n. 4.

4. Parsons: 1939: 127-128: "Of the four Hopi Men's societies, tribal societies into one of which every youth has to be initiated, Singers, Wuwuchim, Agave, and Horn."

5. Stephen: 1936: 25: "They tell me he represents Tai'owa,* the son of the Sun, hailing from a white mountain at the northwest end of the Zuni mountains."

6. Stevenson: 1904: 408: "The second fraternal organization by the Divine Ones was the Newekwe."

7. Ibid: 430: Kokothlanna says, "That is well. Come and live with me and you shall be musician and jester to the Sun Father."

8. Lange: 1968: 229: "The home of the Kwe'rana is in the east; that of Ku-sha'li, though they are more closely associated with the sun, is considered more in the vicinity of Cochiti itself, which is the center of the universe."

9. Stevenson: 1904: 48, n. b.

10. Parsons: 1917: 230: "The first newekwe was called bitsitsi, a name not given to his representative today, however, except when he comes in the molawia ceremonial. [P]ayatemu is another name, according to Stevenson, for bitsitsi, and she gives a legend of his relationship to the Sun.* [B]itsitsi is referred to, I learned, as yatokia payatemu (sun musician)."

11. Stevenson: 1904: 409, n.

12. Cushing: 1896: 433-434: "The flutes sang and sighed as the wind in a wooded canyon whilst still the storm is distant. White mists floated up from the wands of the maidens and mingled with the breath of the flutes over the terraced world-bowl, above which sported the butterflies of Summerland, about the dress of the Rainbow in the strange blue light of the night."

13. Ibid: 442-445. The description is of a water-bringing (Flute) dance that is of the same nature as the Corn Dance and probably produced a conflict in the ceremonial structure at Zuni.

14. Ibid: 443.

15. Parsons: 1939: 439.

16. Cushing: 1896: 443.

17. Ibid: 439.

18. Stephen: 1936: 153-154.

19. Parsons: 1929: 252.

20. Stephen: 1936: 864, 928, 1298: "Tai'owatuh is also another name for Wu'wuchimtuh. Taiowa and Marau are brother and sister and Sun is their father."

21. Parsons: 1939: 294,n. +: ". . . possibly to beautify themselves. Taiowa, their patron spirit being a handsome man."

22. White: 1935: 97-99. Also Parsons: 1939: 410:
   "No longer early in the morning
   do they go outside
   and pray with pollen
   to the Sun Youth."

23. Bunzel: 1932: 860: "[Y]ellow clay is found at Sacred Lake . . . he mixes the ground stone with the dried petals of yellow flowers and Paiyatamu medicine which he gets from the society people. The Paiyatamu medicine is made in the winter during the society meetings. The buttercups and other bright flowers are gathered and dried during the summer. Then in winter the society people invite pretty girls to come and grind. . . .It is never made in the summer unless they run out of it." Ibid: 874: "[I]t is called utea'owe (flower meal) or Paiyatamu medicine. . . .[I]t is made from the petals of yellow and purple flowers. . . . All the butterflies go to the bright-colored flowers and people like to pick them. Therefore they make this medicine with bright flowers. They mix it with the paint they use on the masks and body, to make the dancers beautiful."

24. Webb and Weinstein: 1973: 107, no. 83. Also Stewart, Dockstader, and Wright: 1979: 66, no. M-150; 68-69, no. M-155.

25. Lange: 1968: 175-176.

26. Parsons: 1933: 102: "When the Koyemshi sing hai! hai! and beat on their wooden drum (in which are the wings of black butterflies [Bunzel: 1932: 521]), even girls who

do not care to go to dances are attracted . . . were a wooden drum to be used in corn-grinding for Shalako, it would make the girls 'crazy' (*halishona*), i.e. sexually passionate."

27. Parsons: 1929: 126.

28. Parsons: 1939: 606: [at Sia] "The chief [of the Hunt Society] gives the initiate a corn-ear fetish, a rattle, eagle-wing feathers, the mountain lion image, and the image of Paiyatyamo, Sun Youth."

29. Ibid: 1939; 308, n. *: "There are several cave shrines in Corn Mountain, the large detached mesa three miles east of Zuni. The one I visited was devoted to the heads of prey animals deposited by the Hunters society and to Paiyatemu, the musical patron of the Little Firebrand society."

Chapter Five: The Koyemsi

1. Bunzel: 1932: 954: The Koyemshi are addressed by the society choir by sending them home with a special farewell song which runs as follows: "Our fathers, Molanhaktu, now you are about to go."

2. Parsons: 1939: 973,n. +, 974: "Tachukti means 'ball-on-head' as does the proper Zuni term for the impersonation, Molanhaktu." Parsons also states: "One of the four or five clown types of the Hopi, the Tachukti or Koyimsi, appear in the Shalako and Horned Water Serpent celebrations and at Powamu and are plainly of Zuni provenience. Like the Koyemshi of Zuni, the Koyimsi wear a knobbed mask* and carry a fawnskin bag. The black cloth of the women is worn as kilt or dress; mask and body are painted with pink-ish clay."

3. Parsons: 1925a: 68, fig. 28: "Koyemsi (Ball head, [in] Hopi, *tachōktō*, [in] Tewa, *huntamehlepo*)."

4. Cushing: 1896: 402: "[W]herefore they are called the Ka'yemashi (Husband men of the Ka'ka or sacred drama-dance)." *Also* Parsons: 1939: 340, n. +: "Koyemshi is a nickname (Bunzel) meaning kachina husband, but it spread to Hopi (Koyimsi)." Bunzel does not say it is a nickname; she merely repeats Cushing's statement. However, as is the case with most Zuni personae, they have a real name and a common name. "Koyemshi" appears to be the common name.

5. Parsons: 1939: 340, n. +, cf. fn. 5: "But it spread to Hopi (Koyimsi) and to Keres and Jemez (Gomaiowish, Acoma; Gumeyoish, Laguna, Jemez)." More correctly, the Jemez figure is Gumeyoishi while at Laguna it is Gumeyoish and G'omaiowish at Acoma.

    Also White: 1962: 170: "The Katsina-Gomaiyawic grouping is described by infor-mants as two different and distinct societies, but they always work together. They are so closely associated in fact that it was not until I went over a membership list . . . that I discovered that some were Gomaiyawic, not Katsina. . . . Gomaiyawic may be translated as 'messenger,' or 'scout' (appendix, 312). The Gomaiyawic are katsina who live in Wenimatse." But see the preceding statement: "They have knobs on their heads (see fig. 30) resembling the Koyemshi of Zuñi with whom they have been equated by Parsons and others (cf. Parsons: 1918: 183; Kroeber: 1917: 145, n. 1)."

    Also White:1942: 228: G'omaiowish "appears as a side dancer." Ibid: 231, fig. 18: "Go'maiyawac."

    Also Parsons:1925b: 110: "16. Snake Society *gumeyoishi*. Of these there are several, eight or nine. They are round masks, of the Zuni *koyemshi* type, but in various colors."

    The wearers of these masks walk in single file, singing. They do not make jokes. "Everybody is afraid of them. Even the *k'ats'ana* don't come out when they are out. They come out only in the big dances of the spring (Eastertide?), when the cacique invites them. Informant. *Gumeyoishi* of Arrowhead society and of Fire society (pl. 15, c). Of these there are several. They are exactly like the *koyemshi* masks of Zuni (Hopi, Laguna). Besides, impersonators wear, like the *koyemshi,* black kilts and black neck pieces, and they say 'funny things'! They come out at foot races (as on First Mesa) and at cures, not at dances."

6. Stephen: 1936: 485: "Fifteen Mud-heads (Ta'chukti) with strips of yucca in right hand challenge the youths to race with them, generally giving the youths a start."

7. Informant: "A Koyemsi may replace any kachina. If someone has not had time to practice or to prepare his mask, he can use a Koyemsi mask."

8. Cushing: 1896: 401.

9. Informant: "The Koyemsi are not kachinas. They live near the kachinas in Wenima."

10. Cushing: 1896: 410: "They may not enter K'yau'hliwa [Kothluwala], but they may point the way and tell him K'yak'lu [Kiaklo] how fearlessly, to win into our presence, for as one even of ourselves is he become; yea, and they [Koyemshi] also, save that they stayed themselves for the ages, midway betwixt the living and the dead, by their own rash acts."

11. Parsons: 1917: 235: "In the knobs of the masks are placed bits of soil collected with a little paddle from the tracks around the town. Through this use of human footprints the *koyemshi* have power over the people."

12. Cushing: 1896: 413: Kiaklo, the kachina, says, "Ye shall attend me, for know that ye [the Koyemshi] are to be the guardians of the Ka'ka [kachinas] and tellers of its meanings, and givers of the enjoyment to the children of men."

13. Parsons: 1939: 974: "Like the [Zuni] Koyemshi they [Hopi Koyimsi] have no altar paraphernalia and no fixed organization of chieftaincy or membership."

14. Titiev: 1944: 121.

15. Parsons: 1939: 130: "A peculiar form of trespass is found among all clown groups, Koyemshi excepted." Usually the clowns make the outline of a house in ashes on the ground but occasionally they will make a circle of ashes or meal and capture anyone who strays into it.

16. Stephen: 1936: 423-441: When the Koyemsi come with the Sio Shalako they are part of the ceremony that was borrowed from the Zuni.

17. Informant.

18. Stephen: 1936: 455: "When the Koyi'mse retired, they were given prayer-feathers by the clowns and went to the kachina shrine ledge (under Anawi'ta's house) and made purification and unmasked."

19. Parsons: 1939: 974: The Koyemsi are sprinkled with meal as sacred figures.

20. Stephen: 1936: 169-170: "The leader carried a large Kohonino tray in which were four wood cones, made of greasewood (*suwabko*) and decorated with cloud design (fig. 101a). In his hand he had a rod of wood and eagle feather (fig. 101b). He set the cones up on top of one another near the fireplace about in the middle of the floor. The others danced around to a roaring song with much dramatic action. In the tray they heaped boiled corn ears, beans, etc., then sought for a girl, but there were none in the kiva, so they took a young married woman, brought her to the middle of the floor where she knelt and tried to lift the cones as high as the staff which the leader held beside them."

21. Voth: 1900: AMNH. #73: With reference to the Sio Koyemsi: "While this mask is typically a Zuni, this kachina has long ago been introduced among the Hopi, where in fact it has rapidly taken the place of the similar Hopi kachina [sic]."

22. Stephen: 1936: 169-170.

23. Voth: 1906: CARN #148.

24. Stephen: 1936: 1149: Stephen calls this figure "Ta'chuktu, Ta'chukti, Ta'tachukti, Tatashuktimuh." *Also* Owens: FMNH #148.

25. Voth: 1893 to 1898: FMNH #63689: "The marks in the face with a crook on one end representing sprouting beans."

26. Colton: 1959: 18.

27. Stephen: 1936: 100: "Kih'sha (Cooper's hawk or sparrow hawk) was the first posses-

sor of a *puchkh'u*. He carried it under his wing and hunted rabbits with it. He plucked a feather from each of his wings and fastened them at the marks toward the point. I find much reluctance to tell anything concerning this weapon. It is modeled after the wing of Kih'sha, and referred to as his wing (*masha'adta*)."

28. Parsons: 1939: 1122: "A [Zuni] Koyemshi organization may have antedated the introduction of the Koyemshi mask, possibly a war scout group corresponding to the Red Eyes of Taos or the Quirana of Keres. The special sex taboo imposed on Koyemshi point to a sometime war character, which among the Gomaiowish of Acoma is still conspicuous."

29. Stevenson: 1880-1884: SNM, no. 41975.

30. Voth: 1893-1898: FMNH. #63681.

31. Colton: 1959: 83: "Tiponi is a symbol of what the Hopi call the 'mother of all.' Every village has one, as do the principal priests and chiefs of all fraternities. . . . In all ceremonies these images will have their places in front of the altar in each kiva, especially in Wuwuchim time in November and for the Soyal Ceremony in December. At those times, every man who has one will bring it into his kiva so that it may receive some pahos, or prayer plumes."

32. Harvey: 1951: ms.

33. Stephen: 369, 1236: "[T]he dance director (*kükü'ina*) in the centre." "kükü'ina (1) the kachina personator who stands in the centre of the line of kachina and starts the song and step and from whom the others take their time."

34. Informant.

35. Titiev: 1944: 220-221.

36. Wright: 1977: 45.

37. Informant.

38. Titiev: 1944: 117: "In each kiva, one or two men then dress in complete kachina costumes, choosing whatever impersonation they prefer."

39. Voth: 1906: CARN. #3165/6.

40. Hieb: 1972: 138: ". . . may appear . . . as a warrior *koyemsi* . . . who warns and later punished the clowns."

41. Stephen: 1936: 1230: "kih'po . . . war cry."

42. Informant.

43. Stephen: 1936: 199-200: Although he describes the replacement of the Tungwub by the Koyemsi in detail he does not call it a Kipok Koyemsi.

44. Informant. *Also* Harvey: 1951: ms.

45. Ellis: #737.

46. Informant.

47. Voth: 1896: FMNH #66169. *Also* Voth: 1905: CARN #3180.

48. Informant.

49. Stephen: 1936: 192-201: Tumash and her two sons were out in the village of Walpi, as Stephen mentions them on both the second (ibid, 192) and third (ibid, 194) days in February 1893; but he has this to say about the fourth day (ibid, 198): "The children are to be flogged this sunset in the court, after which they must not eat salt or flesh for four days, then they may look upon kachina and wi'mi in kivas. The Horn kiva people told me there would be no Tungwub kachina at Walpi because there are no Walpi children to be qualified, only one from Tewa (Numpe'yo's boy), hence the Tungwub would come from Tewa. In Horn kiva Wi'nuta explains that the Tewa children will be initiated at Tewa . . . Takala in Horn kiva is to represent Tungwub kachina. . . . He wears a clown (Ta'chukti) mask (fig. 119) with a black band across the eyes, parroquet feather plume on the crown, turkey tail feathers radiating horizontal from the crown toward the rear

[after the fashion of the Tungwub kachina]; a cloth shirt, the white woolen blanket with red and black border as kilt girded with the big belt, yellow clay on his legs, tortoise rattle below each knee, moccasins black with red heel fringe . . . a bunch of yucca in each hand, butts in front."

50. Informant.

51. Informant.

52. Stephen: 1936:162.

53. Informant.

54. Fewkes: 1903: 46-47: "One of the naked men, a mudhead, wearing the knobbed cloth bag, stepped forward and grasped one of the serpent effigies by the neck. He pretended to wrestle with the snake, and for a time was successful, but at last the man was overcome and sent sprawling to the floor. Then another advanced to the conflict, and he too was thrown down. A youthful mudhead made a like attempt and mounted the effigy, riding on its neck as if on horseback."

55. Voth: 1900: FMNH #63826.

56. Informant. *Also* Hegemann: 1920: Specimen, Museum of Northern Arizona. *Also* Laboratory of Anthropology #25555/12.

57. A bull-roarer is a thin, wooden slat suspended on a string that, when whirled about the head, produces a roaring sound believed to sound like thunder.

58. Maxwell Museum, no. 64.87.1.

59. Geertz and Lomatuwayma: 1987: 147-175: The Koyemsi can be presented as the Koyemsihoya who are puppets and are considered to be living beings.

60. Informant.

Chapter Six: The Piptuyakyamu

1. Stephen: 1936: 1280.

2. Ibid: 332.

3. Ibid: 158.

4. Ibid: 332.

5. Ibid: 385

6. Ibid: 387.

7. Ibid.

8. Barrett: 1911: #3916.

9. Stephen: 1936: 169, 506.

SPECIMEN NOTES

The author wishes to acknowledge the following sources whose carvings, performances, paintings, and other artistic representations of clowns and kachinas were a valuable resource while preparing the illustrations used in this book. (Figure numbers not listed are generalized and have no recognized sources.)

Figure 2—The University of Colorado Museum, catalog number 16214, Wolle Coll.; also Second Mesa 1937; also Maxwell Museum of Anthropology, catalog number 63.34.248, ca. 1960-1970.

Figure 3—Gallery.

Figure 4—Obrecht Collection, Wilfred Tewawina, Moencopi.

Figures 6 and 7—*Museum fur Volkerkunde* (Berlin/Dahlem), catalog number IVB-5132 and IVB-5133, collected by Thomas Keam prior to 1900.

Figure 8—Maxwell Museum of Anthropology, catalog number 64.61.203, collected 1960-1970.

Figure 9—The American Museum of Natural History, catalog number 50.9498, collected in 1904; also Southwest Museum, catalog number 421-G-106, collected by G.W. James.

Figures 10 and 11—Museum of New Mexico/Lab. of Anthro., catalog number 1357/12 and 1358/12, collected by H.R.Voth 1893-1910.

Figure 12—Smithsonian Institution.

Figure 13—Collection unknown, possibly collected by H.R. Voth 1893-1898.

Figure 14—*Arizona's Colorful Indians,* by Ray Manley and Howard Kinney, Arizona Highways, 1967.

Figure 15—Smithsonian Institution, catalog number 22939, collected by Major John Wesley Powell in 1885.

Figures 16 and 17—Carnegie Museum of Natural History, catalog number 3165/79 (#62) and 3165/103, collected by H.R.Voth 1898-1906.

Figure 19—Stephen: 1936, fig. 282, performance.

Figure 20—The Heard Museum, catalog number 36, Duane Dishta painting.

Figure 21—The Heard Museum, possibly catalog number Ho-F-46.

Figure 23—Judson Ball, catalog number JB-02767-19.

Figure 22—Field Museum of Natural History, catalog number 65731, collected by H.R.Voth, Oraibi, 1893-1898; also the American Museum of Natural History, catalog number 50.9488 (#216), collected by H.R.Voth 1905-1910.

Figure 24—Museum of New Mexico/Lab. of Anthro., catalog number 52791/12, purchased in the 1940s.

Figure 25—Matilda Coxe Stevenson, p.106, 23rd Annual Report, BAE.

Figure 26—The Heard Museum, Duane Dishta painting; also *Kachinas of the Zuni,* pl. 48b, Duane Dishta.

Figures 27 and 28—Stephen: 1936, pp.360-64, 1893 performance at Sichomovi.

Figure 30—Field Museum of Natural History Archives, drawing collected by H.R.Voth in 1896; also private collection.

Figure 31—Museum of New Mexico/Lab. of Anthro., catalog number 53188/12, collected during 1890s.

Figure 32—Museum of New Mexico/Lab. of Anthro., catalog number 1364/12, collected by H.R.Voth, Oraibi, 1893-1898.

Figure 33—Performance, Bakabi. 1984.

Figure 35—Maxwell Museum of Anthropology, catalog number 73.9.16, collected 1960-1970; also Museum of New Mexico/Lab. of Anthro., catalog number 1275/12, collected by H.R.Voth, Oraibi, 1893-1898.

Figure 36—Performance/private collection, 1984.

Figure 37—*Santa Ana,* by Leslie A.White, fig.8, p.126, 1942.

Figures 38 and 39—*San Felipe,* by Leslie A.White, fig.2d and 2c, p.17, 1932.

Figure 40—*Zia,* by Leslie A.White, fig.18, p.167, 1962.

Figure 41—*Isleta,* by Esther Goldfrank, p.183, 1962; also Elsie Clews Parsons, page 334, 1974.

Figure 42—*Santo Domingo,* by Chas. H. Lange, fig. 11, 1979.

Figure 43—*San Ildefonso,* by Gilbert Atencio, #59, pp.182-202, 1956; *Tryntje,* by Van Ness Seymour, 1988.

Figure 44—Museum of New Mexico/Lab. of Anthro., catalog number 25552/12.

Figure 45—Maxwell Museum of Anthropology, catalog number 64.61.81, collected by D. Maxwell ca. 1960.

Figure 46—Maxwell Museum of Anthropology, catalog number 73.9.23, collected ca. 1960-1970; also C.E.Smith Museum, catalog number 61, collected by Mr. and Mrs. J. Lee, First Mesa, 1950-1970.

Figure 47—Gallery.

Figure 48—Gallery.

Figure 49—Private collection.

Figure 50—C.E.Smith Museum, collected by Mr. & Mrs. J.Lee, First Mesa, 1950-1970.

Figure 51—Performance, Mishongnovi, 1966

Figure 52—Carnegie Museum of Natural History, catalog number 3253 (#106), collected by H.R.Voth 1893-1898; also *Museum fur Volkerkunde* (Berlin/Dahlem), catalog number IVB 5123, collected by Thomas Keam before 1900.

Figure 53—Smithsonian Institution, catalog number 41974, collected by Col. James Stevenson 1880-1884.

Figure 54—Field Museum of Natural History, catalog number 65681, collected by H.R.Voth 1893-1898; also Smithsonian Institution, catalog number 41975, collected by Col. James Stevenson 1880-1884.

Figure 55—Milwaukee Public Museum, catalog number 8379/3101, collected by Samuel Barrett in 1911.

Figure 56—Carnegie Museum of Natural History, catalog number 1683/24, collected by Voorhies at Toreva in 1898.

Figures 57, 60, and 62—*Zuni Kachinas,* by Ruth Bunzel, pl. 23a, p. 946, 1932; also the Brooklyn Museum, catalog numbers 03.325.4602, 03.325.4602, and 03.325.4601, collected by Stewart Culin in 1903.

Figure 58—*Zuni Kachinas,* by Ruth Bunzel, pl. 23a, p. 946, 1932.

Figures 59, 61, and 63-66—*Zuni Kachinas*, by Ruth Bunzel, pl. 23a, p. 946, 1932; also private collection, New York, catalog numbers SK7, SK7, SK12, SK14, SK 13, and SK13.

Figure 67—San Diego Museum of Man, catalog number 50, collected by R.Lovett 1960-1970.

Figure 68—Maxwell Museum of Anthropology, catalog number 73.9.31, collected by D.Maxwell ca. 1950-1960; also performance, Shungopovi, 1956.

Figure 70—Maxwell Museum of Anthropology, catalog number 64.61.115, collected by D.Maxwell ca. 1950; also performance, Shungopovi, 1957 and 1987.

Figure 71—Performance, Shungopovi, 1987.

Figure 72—Private collection, collected by Florence Ellis in 1966; also performance, Shungopovi, 1965 and 1966.

Figure 73—Field Museum of Natural History, catalog number 82781; also Museum Shop, Museum of Northern Arizona, Flagstaff, 1965.

Figure 74—Performance, Shungopovi, 1989.

Figure 75—Carnegie Museum of Natural History, catalog number 1683/41, collected by Voorhies, Toreva, 1898.

Figure 76—Stephen: 1936, fig. 119, performance ca. 1890.

Figure 77—Performance, Shungopovi, 1953.

Figure 78—Museum of New Mexico/Lab. of Anthro., catalog number 1372/12, collected by H.R.Voth.

Figure 79—Private collection, catalog number K-3.

Figure 80—Maxwell Museum of Anthropology, catalog number 88.65.51, collected by D. Maxwell ca. 1950-1960; also Museum of Northern Arizona Show, Joseph Robinson, Bakabi, 1965.

Figure 81—Museum of Northern Arizona Show, Wayne Taylor, Shungopovi, 1956, and Jennifer Masawytewa, Mishongnovi, 1966.

Figure 82—Museum Shop, Museum of Northern Arizona, Flagstaff, ca. 1960-1965.

Figure 83—Museum Shop, Museum of Northern Arizona, Flagstaff.

Figure 84—C.E. Smith Museum, catalog number 70, collected by Mr. & Mrs. J.Lee, First Mesa, 1950-1970; also Museum of New Mexico/Lab of Anthro., catalog number 44816, collected by H.Volz ca. 1900.

Figure 85—Fred Harvey Collection, catalog number FH 93iCL; also Museum of New Mexico/Lab of Anthro., collected by Thomas Keam, First Mesa, ca. 1890.

Figure 86—Field Museum of Natural History, catalog number 65826, collected by H.R.Voth, Oraibi, 1893-1898; also performance, Shungopovi, 1952.

Figure 87—Museum of Northern Arizona, catalog number 2277/E.2292, collected by E. C. Hegemann, Oraibi, ca.1920; formerly from the Carlos Viera Coll.

Figure 88—Private collection, collected by F. Ellis.

Figure 89—Museum Shop, Museum of Northern Arizona, Flagstaff, Herman Shelton, 1977.

Figure 90—C.E. Smith Museum, catalog number 167, collected by Mr. and Mrs. J.Lee, First Mesa, 1950-1970; also performance, Shungopovi, 1985.

Figures 91 and 92—Stephen: 1936, p. 367 and 368, performance.

Figure 93—Performance, Shungopovi, 1989.

Figure 94—Edmund Nequatewa, catalog number 61, Colton, 1959.

Figure 95—Edmund Nequatewa, catalog number 252, Colton, 1959.

Figure 96—Performance, Hotevilla, 1967.

Figure 97—Maxwell Museum of Anthropology, catalog number 64.61.224, collected by D. Maxwell ca. 1950-1960.

Figure 98—Museum of Northern Arizona Show, Sharon Lee Sockyma, 1966, and Henry Shelton, 1965.

GLOSSARY

A-Ahltu: The Two-Horned Society of the Hopi men

Acoma: A Keresan village of the western Pueblos

Ahöl Mana: A kachina maiden who accompanies the chief kachina, Ahöla

A'mitolan Te'poula: A spring near Zuni

Anktioni: Springtime repeat dances of the Hopi

Atosle: An Ogre kachina of the Hopi

Bitsitsi: Musician and jester for the clowns at Zuni; an alternate name for Payatamu

Chama River: A tributary of the northern Rio Grande

Chaveyo: A fierce Hopi kachina

Chilikomato: One of the Hopi racing kachinas

Cochiti: An eastern, or Rio Grande Keresan, pueblo

Choqapölö: A mud-throwing kachina of the Hopi

Chosbusi Kachina: Turquoise-Ear-Pendant kachina, a warrior against the Hopi clowns

Choshuhuwa: The Bluebird Snare kachina of the Hopi

Dyu'weni: A Cochiti kachina

G'o'maiowish: The Acoma form of the Koyemshi

Go'maiyawash: The Santa Ana form of the Koyemshi

Go'maiyawish: The Zia form of the Koyemshi

Gowawaima: *See* Kowawaima

Gumeyiosh: The Laguna form of the Koyemshi

Gumeyoishi: The Jemez form of the Koyemshi

Hahai-i Wuhti: Mother of all Hopi kachinas

Heheya Aumutaka: The uncle of the Hopi Heheya kachina

Hewa Hewa: A Zuni group of buffoons associated with the Newekwe Society

Hisat: Old or ancient

Ho-e: A clown for the kachinas; *see also* Wo-e

Hopi: The westernmost people of the western pueblos; a Shoshonean language

Hopok: Eastern, or an eastern kachina
Huhuwa: The Cross-Legged kachina of the Hopi
Isleta: An eastern, or Rio Grande Tiwan, pueblo

Jemez: An eastern, or Rio Grande Towan, pueblo

Kaisale: The Hopi version of the winter clown, or Kwirena
Kaisale Mana: The female aspect of the winter clown, or Kwirena
Keresan: A linguistic branch among the Pueblo people
Kipok Koyemsi: War Leader Mudhead, or Warrior Against the
    Clowns
Köcha Tsutskut: White clowns among the Hopi
Köcha Omau-u Tsuku: A White Cloud clown among the Hopi
Kokopelli: A phallic, hump-backed, flute-playing kachina
Kokopell' Mana: The female version of the hump-backed, flute-
    playing kachina
Koshari: The summer clowns of the eastern pueblos; also called
    Kusha'li, K'shale, Kosairi, Kaishali
Kossa: Both of the winter and summer clowns among the eastern
    pueblos; a generic name
Kothluwala: The sacred lake, home of the kachinas at Zuni
Ko-tsutskutu: The white clowns of the Hopi
Koyala: An alternate name for the Koshari
Koyemsi: The ball-headed personae of the Hopi; a Mudhead
Koyemsihoya: A ceremonial puppet of the Koyemsi found among
    the Hopi
Koyemsi Mana: The female Mudhead, or Ball-on-Head girl
Koyemshi: The ball-headed personae of the Zuni
Kowawaima: The kachina resting place to the south
Kuikuinaka: A Koyemsi who is the representative of Muyingwa,
    who acts as the starter for a dance
Kuwan: Colorful
Kuwan Koshari: Colorful summer clown, or Hano Glutton
Kwakwantu: The One-Horned men's society among the Hopi
Kwikwilyaka: a mocking kachina among the Hopi
Kwirena: The winter clowns of the eastern pueblos

Laguna: The easternmost of the western pueblos
Lutkyanakwe: Ash Spring at Zuni

Mamzrau: A women's society at Hopi
Masau-u: Hopi earth deity
Mastop: A Third Mesa Chief kachina at Hopi

126

Moencopi: The farthest-west Hopi pueblo
Moiety: One of two equal parts; a kinship division among many
    pueblos
Molanhakto: The proper name of the Koyemshi at Zuni
Molawia: An important Zuni ceremony
Momo: The Bee kachina among the Hopi
Mong Koyemsi: A Chief Mudhead among the Hopi
Mongwi: A Hopi chief
Mongwu: Great Horned Owl kachina among the Hopi
Muyingwu: Hopi Germination God in the Underworld

Naka: Hopi term for earrings
Nakwakwosi: A prayer feather among the Hopi
Nambé: An eastern, or Rio Grande Tewa, pueblo
Na'somta Tsutskut: Hopi Hair-Knot clowns
Natukvika: A Hopi kachina who resembles part of a Koshari
Nepaiyatemu: The informal clown society of the Zuni
Newekwe: The formal Zuni clown society

Omau-u Humikumi: Clouds Rising kachinas of the Hopi
O-oto Tsuku: Prairie Dog clowns of the Hopi
Oshatsh Paiyatamu: The Sun Youth at Acoma and other Keresan
    pueblos
O-tsukut: Clown initiates among the Hopi; Red clowns

Pachok'china: The Hopi Cocklebur kachina, one of the racing kachinas
Paho: Prayerstick used by the Hopi; prayer offering
Palhik'o: A Mamzrau, or women's society dance among the Hopi
Palhik' Mana: Water-Drinking Girl of the Mamzrau society among the
    Hopi
Palölökong: The Plumed Water Serpent of the Hopi
Pal Ölökongti: The Plumed Water Serpent ceremony among the Hopi
Paiyakyamu: The Kossa of the Rio Grande; clowns comprised of the
    Koshari and Kwirena at Hopi
Paiyatam': The Red-Striped clowns among the Hopi
Paiyatamhoya: The open-eyed, Red-Striped clowns of Second Mesa
Paiyatamu: The supernatural patron of clowns, the Sun Youth; also
    Tapaiyachiamu, or clown society
Paiyata-um Kachina: A kachina derived from the Cochiti Pai'yat- yama
    kachina
Pai'yat-yama: A Cochiti kachina; a dance pole
Pashiwawash: A racing ritual of the Hopi
Picuris: An eastern, or Rio Grande Tiwan, pueblo

Piptuyakyamu: The informal buffoons among the Hopi

Pitkuna: A ceremonial kilt used by the Hopi

Pöökanghoya: The elder of the Two Little War Gods among the Hopi

Powak: A Hopi witch

Powak Koyemsi: A wizard or magician Mudhead; the term also means witch

Powalunga: A witch's ceremony

Powamu: A late-winter ceremony among the Hopi, performed to prepare for the growing season

Powamu Koyemsi: The Mudhead who brings presents and bean sprouts to the children during Powamu

Powamu So-Aum Wuhti: A kachina-style "woman" who appears in Hopi kivas during Powamu

Puukanghoya: *See* Pöökanghoya

Quirena: *See* Kwirena

Qöqöle: A chief kachina among the Hopi

Sakwa Koshari: The blue-bodied form of the Hano clown, or Koshari

Sakwats Mana: One of the female kachinas who appears as a runner among the Hopi

Sandia: An eastern, or Rio Grande Tiwan, pueblo

San Ildefonso: An eastern, or Rio Grande Tewan, pueblo

San Jose River: A tributary of the middle Rio Grande

San Juan: An eastern, or Rio Grande Tewan, pueblo

Santa Ana: An eastern, or Rio Grande Keresan, pueblo

Santa Clara: An eastern, or Rio Grande Keresan, pueblo

Santo Domingo: An eastern, or Rio Grande Keresan, pueblo

Shiwannakwe: The Rain Society of the Zuni

Sho'kona: A flute with a large, bell-shaped end

Shoshone: An extensive Native American linguistic stock, to which the Hopi belong

Shungopovi: A Second Mesa village on the Hopi Reservation

Shun'lekaiya: A mesa near the base of Towayalanne Mesa, southeast of Zuni

Si-Chaiz Tsuku: Yellow Cloud clowns among the Hopi

Sikya Heheya: The yellow Heheya of Second Mesa among the Hopi

Sikya Koshari: The yellow-bodied Koshari among the Hopi

Sikya Tsutskutu: The yellow clowns of the Hopi

Sipapuni: A place of Emergence from previous worlds; also called the sipapu

Sosoyoktu: The generic name for all of the Ogre kachinas among the Hopi

Soyok' Wuhti: The Hopi Ogre Woman kachina

Tachukti: The indigenous Hopi Ball-On-Head; also called Tatci'oktu, Tatci'oqtu, or Tatsi'oktu

Taiowa: The supernatural Son of the Sun among the Hopi

Talasunga: Another name for the Piptuka on Hopi Second Mesa

Talavai-i: A generic term for all Morning kachinas, or specifically, the Morning Kachina

Taos: An eastern, or Rio Grande Towan, pueblo

Tasaf Yeibichai: The Navajo Grandfather kachina of the Hopi

Tasavu: A pseudo-clown representing the Navajo, found among the Hopi

Tataukyamu: The men's Singer Society among the Hopi

Tatcimu Koyemsi: A ball-playing Mudhead, or Koyemsi, among the Hopi

Tatsi'oktu: The term for the indigenous Hopi Ball-On-Head on Hopi Third Mesa; *see* Tachukti

Te'nat'sali: A medicinal plant at Zuni

Tesuque: An eastern, or Rio Grande Tewan, pueblo

Tewa: A linguistic branch of the eastern Pueblos, or the inhabitants of Hano on First Mesa among the Hopi

Tihu: A small carved wooden image of a kachina among the Hopi

Tiponi: A Hopi object symbolizing power or control, usually made of corn and feathers

Tiwa: A linguistic branch of the Rio Grande, or eastern pueblos

Toson Koyemsi: The Sweet-Cornmeal-Tasting Mudhead of the Hopi

Towa: The northernmost linguistic branch of the eastern, or Rio Grande, pueblos

Towayalanne: A large, distinctive mesa southeast of Zuni; also called Corn Mountain

Tsukuhoya: The term used for a boy being initiated into the clowns

Tsukuwimkya: The generic term for Hopi clowns

Ts'un'tatabo'sh: The Kwirena at the pueblo of Jemez

Tumash: The Crow Mother kachina from First Mesa among the Hopi

Tungwup: The Whipper kachinas from First Mesa among the Hopi

Tuvé Koyemsi: The replacement Koyemsi of the Hopi

Wenima: The interpueblo name for the kachinas' home in the west

Wo-e: Another name for the Ho-e, a clown for the kachinas among the Hopi

Wuhti Tsuku: A Hopi woman clown

Wuwuchim: A Hopi men's society and an important ceremonial

Yatokia Paiyatamu: the Musician to the Sun at Zuni
Yoche: Hopi term for an Apache
Yohozro Wuhti: Comb-Hair-Upwards kachina among the Hopi

Zia: An eastern, or Rio Grande Keresan, pueblo
Zuni: A distinctive western Pueblo people and their village

BIBLIOGRAPHY

Bandelier, Adolph A. F. 1890. *The Delight Makers*. Dodd, Mead and Co., New York, New York.

Barrett, Samuel. 1911. "Notes. Expedition of the Milwaukee Public Museum to the Hopi." Milwaukee Public Museum, Milwaukee, Wisconsin.

Beaglehole, Ernest, and Pearl Beaglehole. 1935. "Hopi of Second Mesa." American Anthropological Association, *Memoirs*, vol. 44. Menasha, Wisconsin.

Bunzel, Ruth. 1932. "Zuni Kachinas." Bureau of American Ethnology, *47th Annual Report*. Washington, D.C.

Colton, Harold S. 1959. *Hopi Kachina Dolls with a Key to Their Identification*. The University of New Mexico Press, Albuquerque.

Cushing, Frank Hamilton. 1896. "Outlines of Zuñi Creation Myths." Bureau of American Ethnology, *13th Annual Report*. Washington, D.C.

Fewkes, J. Walter. 1892. "A Few Summer Ceremonials at Tusayan Pueblos." *Journal of American Ethnology and Archaeology*, vol. 2. The Riverside Press, Cambridge.

———. 1903. "Hopi Katcinas Drawn by Native Artists." Bureau of American Ethnology, *21st Annual Report*. Washington, D.C.

Geertz, Armin W. and Michael Lomatuway'ma. 1987. *Children of Cottonwood: Piety and Ceremonialism in Hopi Indian Puppetry*. University of Nebraska Press, Lincoln.

Goldfrank, Esther Schiff. 1927. "The Social and Ceremonial Organization of Cochiti." American Anthropological Association, *Memoirs*, no. 33. Menasha, Wisconsin.

———. 1962. "Isleta Paintings." Bureau of American Ethnology, *Bulletin 181*. Smithsonian Institution, Washington D.C.

Harvey, Byron, III. 1951. manuscript.

———. 1971 "Ritual in Pueblo Art: Hopi Life in Hopi Painting." Museum of the American Indian, Heye Foundation, New York, New York.

Hieb, Louis Albert. 1972. "The Hopi Ritual Clown: Life as it should not be." Ph.D. diss., Princeton University, Princeton, New Jersey.

Lange, Charles H. 1968. *Cochiti: A New Mexico Pueblo: Past and Present*. Southern Illinois University Press, Carbondale.

———. 1979. "Santo Domingo Pueblo." *Handbook of the American Indians*, vol. 9: 379-389. Smithsonian Institution, Washington, D.C.

Mindeleff, Victor. 1891. "A Study of Pueblo Architecture: Tusayan and Cibola." Bureau of American Ethnology, *8th Annual Report*. Washington, D.C.

Oxford English Dictionary. 1971. 2 vols. Oxford Press, New York, New York.

Parsons, Elsie Clews. 1917. "Notes on Zuñi." American Anthropological Association, *Memoirs*, vol. 4, nos. 3, 4, pts. I, II. Menasha, Wisconsin.

———. 1918. "Winter and Summer Dance Series in Zuñi in 1918." *Publications in American Archaeology and Ethnology*, vol. 17. University of California, Berkeley.

———. 1920. "Notes on Ceremonialism at Laguna." *Anthropological Papers of American Museum of Natural History*, vol. XIX, pt. IV. New York, New York.

———. 1923. "The Hopi Wöwöchim Ceremony in 1920." *American Anthropologist*, n.s., vol. 25, no. 2. Menasha, Wisconsin.

———. 1925a. "A Pueblo Indian Journal, 1920-1921." American Anthropological Association, *Memoirs*, no. 32. Menasha, Wisconsin.

———. 1925b. *The Pueblo of Jemez*. Department of Archaeology, Phillips Academy, Yale University Press. Andover, Massachusetts.

———. 1926. "The Ceremonial Calendar of the Tewa of Arizona." *American Anthropologist*, n. s., vol. 28, no. I. Menasha, Wisconsin.

———. 1929. "The Social Organization of the Tewa of New Mexico." American Anthropological Association, *Memoirs*, no. 36. Menasha, Wisconsin.

———. 1932. "The Pueblo of Isleta." Bureau of American Ethnology, *47th Annual Report*. Washington, D.C.

———. 1933. "Hopi and Zuñi Ceremonialism." American Anthropological Association, *Memoirs*, vol. 39. Menasha, Wisconsin.

———. 1936. "Hopi Journal of Alexander M. Stephen." *Contributions to Anthropology*, vol. 23 (2 vols.). Columbia University, New York, New York.

———. 1939. *Pueblo Indian Religion* (2 vols.). The University of Chicago Press, Chicago, Illinois.

Seymour, Tryntje Van Ness. 1988. "When the Rainbow Touches Down." *Gilbert Atencio* #55, 1956. The Heard Museum, University of Washington Press, Phoenix, Arizona, and Seattle.

Stephen, Alexander M. 1936. "Hopi Journal." edited by Elsie Clews Parsons. *Contributions to Anthropology*, vol. 23 (2 vols.). Columbia University, New York, New York.

Stevenson, Matilda Coxe. 1904. "The Zuñi Indians." Bureau of American Ethnology, *23rd Annual Report*. Washington, D.C.

Thompson, Laura. 1950. *Culture In Crisis: A Study of the Hopi Indians*. Harper & Bros., New York, New York.

Titiev, Mischa. 1944. "Old Oraibi: A Study of the Hopi Indians of Third Mesa." *Papers of the Peabody Museum of American Archaeology and Ethnology*, vol. XXII, no. I. Harvard University, Cambridge, Massachusetts.

———. 1972. *The Hopi Indians of Old Oraibi: Change and Continuity*. The University of Michigan Press, Ann Arbor.

Voth, H. R. 1901. "The Oraibi Powamu Ceremony." *Anthropological Series*, vol. 3, no. 2. Field Museum of Chicago, Chicago, Illinois.

———. 1898. Arizona History Foundation, V-53. Tempe, Arizona.

Webb, William, and Robert A. Weinstein. 1973. *Dwellers at the Source: Southwestern Indian Photographs of A. C. Vroman, 1895-1904*. Natural History Museum of Los Angeles County, Grossman Publishers, Los Angeles, California, and New York, New York.

White, Leslie A. 1932a "The Pueblo of San Felipe." American Anthropological Association, *Memoirs*, no. 38. Menasha, Wisconsin.

———. 1932b. "The Acoma Indians." Bureau of American Ethnology, *47th Annual Report*. Washington, D.C.

———. 1942. "The Pueblo of Santa Ana, New Mexico." American Anthropological Association, *Memoirs*, no. 60. Menasha, Wisconsin.

———. 1962a. "New Material from Acoma." Bureau of American Ethnology, *Bulletin 136*. Smithsonian Institution, Washington, D.C.

———. 1962b. "The Pueblo of Sia, New Mexico." Bureau of American Ethnology, *Bulletin 184*. Smithsonian Institution, Washington, D.C.

Wright, Barton. 1973. *Kachinas, A Hopi Artist's Documentary*. Northland Press, Flagstaff, Arizona.

———. 1979. "The Year of the Hopi: Paintings and Photographs by Joseph Mora, 1904-1906." Smithsonian Institution Traveling Exhibition Service, Washington, D.C..

INDEX

ABOUT THE AUTHOR

Barton Wright has been recognized by his peers in the scientific community as a leading authority on Hopi Kachinas. He has been a director of scientific research at the San Diego Museum of Man, a curator of the Museum of Northern Arizona, and an archaeologist for the Amerind Foundation. His publications include *Pueblo Shields, Hopi Kachinas: The Complete Guide to Collecting Kachina Dolls,* and *The Unchanging Hopi.* He lives in Phoenix, Arizona, with his wife, Margaret.